Border
Voices

ABRIDGED

An Anthology from
Borders Writers' Forum

Cover photographs:
Front – close by Cleikimmin Junction, Ancrum
(Tony Parkinson)
Back – Leaderfoot (Drygrange) Viaduct
(Campbell Hutcheson)

This anthology is a taster of Borders Writers' Forum members' writing on the theme of 'bridge' in the Borders and beyond, whether physical, emotional, psychological or metaphorical.

Further information on the Forum and its members can be found at: www.borderswritersforum.org.uk and on Facebook

Borders Voices ABRIDGED
An Anthology from Borders Writers' Forum
Copyright © Borders Writers' Forum April 2017

Copyright © for photographs remains with individual members' submissions or Tony Parkinson.

All rights reserved
No part of this publication may be reproduced, stored in a retrieval system, or transmitted in any form or by any means, without the prior permission in writing of the publisher, nor be otherwise circulated in any form of binding or cover other than that in which it is published and without a similar condition including this condition being imposed on the subsequent purchaser.

British Library Cataloguing-in-Publication Data
A CIP catalogue record for this book is available from the British Library

ISBN: 978-0-9926261-5-0

Cover design: Sarah Thompson Text pages: Tony Parkinson

Published by:
Borders Writers' Forum
c/o Double Elephant Associates
Orchard Cottage, Lanton
Jedburgh, Scottish Borders TD8 6SX
www.borderswritersforum.org.uk

Border
Voices
ABRIDGED

Introduction

As one of the artists on the *Working the Tweed* project, I learned from scientists at Tweed Forum that the Tweed is one of the most dendritic rivers in Europe. The most water-tentacled river, right here on our doorstep – who knew? Kate Foster's illustration of the Tweed river catchment revealed our region as not some random map-zone penned by an official, but a living water-lung shaped by hills and sea. With all this water everywhere, it follows that the Borders has a lot of bridges, and some of them make an appearance here. In this timely new anthology by Borders Writers' Forum, you'll find bridges large and small, hidden and brazen, literal, metaphorical, and a bit of both, in local landscapes and landscapes of the mind, striding arches making ways. Bridges are all about connecting what's apart, and what better theme, in this time of binaries and false divisions? And from a place where two countries meet and fuse with no visible join? Enjoy this collection of fine Borders writing, and these clear voices from a refreshing range of viewing points.

Jules Horne
Literature Advocate, CABN

Border Voices

ABRIDGED

Bridges to Heaven
by Antony Chessell

A serpent with three humps, thrust up and turned to stone by some primordial spell? Perhaps an imaginative interpretation of an oblique view of the 'Bridge to Heaven' at Stow of Wedale in the Scottish Borders because, sideways on, it is clearly not a monster but a three-arched packhorse bridge, the main arch spanning the Gala Water with two subsidiary arches ready to take the frequent flood water. It was built by public subscription in the 17th century, which gives rise to its other name, the 'Subscription Bridge'. The low parapets allowed wide horse-drawn loads to cross the river without obstruction, very necessary when Stow was solely a farming community. It was the construction of the bridge at the lowest possible crossing point of the Gala that led to Stow's prosperity by linking the village with the Galashiels to Edinburgh road, which, at the time, ran along the other side of the valley. Transport links became even more important with the advent of the railway and when Stow became known as a centre for spinning and weaving at the start of the industrial revolution. A practical structure it may have been, but the bridge's beautifully constructed narrow-depth stone arches with their neatly interlocking voussoirs, must always have attracted admiring attention. Now, the turfed carriageway between the parapets adds to its appearance.

The derivation of Stow is probably from Anglo-Saxon, meaning a meeting place or a holy place and *Wedale* possibly comes from *wa* or *wœ* and *dal* meaning a dale or a valley of woe. Why it was a valley of woe is unknown but maybe it is because Stow is rumoured to have been the site of one of King Arthur's victories over the Saxons, certainly a woeful defeat for them. But it might not have been a dale of woe if *we* derives from *wiche* meaning shrine; the interpretation would then be, valley of the shrine. These distant folklore memories also record that King Arthur founded the first church here, dedicated to the Virgin Mary and endowed it with fragments said to be from the True Cross. This might have been a chapel next to St. Mary's Well to the south of the village but whether or not this was so, it is thought that Christianity reached the area by the 7th century and there are surviving records for the well going back to the early 9th century. In 1242, a new church was built next to the palace of the bishops of St. Andrews who had owned the church and the lands around since 1018 when Lothian was ceded to the Scots. Another new church was built in the 15th century and largely rebuilt in the 17th century but, in 1876, the church that we see today was built on a new site, a short distance to the south. The packhorse bridge crosses the Gala opposite the present Stow St. Mary of Wedale and Heriot Church and not far away from the site of the previous medieval churches. So it is not surprising that it acquired the name, 'Bridge to Heaven', even more so as it was built with consecrated stones taken from the old churches.

About thirty miles to the east is a much more modest bridge with only one arch, carrying a farm track across the fledgling River Leet, east of Ravelaw Farm and just north of the village of Whitsome. It seems surprising that such a very small but well-constructed bridge is to be found in this location between two fields when a ford might have served just as well. This bridge also has low random rubble parapets and coping stones to allow for the easy passage of wide-topped loads, but the barrel arch with its very precise voussoirs hints at a one-time, higher status. John Bartholomew's map of 1797, shows that there was once a hamlet of Ravelaw to the east of the present farm. It was here that the Rev. Henry Erskine (1624-1696) lived and preached after he was expelled from his parish of Cornhill-on-Tweed on St. Bartholomew's Day 1662 following the Act of Uniformity of that year. The Act required all Church of England services to be conducted in accordance with the rites and ceremonies in the Book of Common Prayer and for all ministers to be ordained by recognised bishops. As a result, nearly 2000 clergymen left the Church of England in what was known as the Great Ejection and the Rev. Erskine first of all found solace over the Border at his birthplace of Dryburgh. Then, after further conflict with the authorities over church procedures, which saw him imprisoned on the Bass Rock and elsewhere, he lived at Monilaws [sic] near Branxton in Northumberland and then at Ravelaw, before eventually being appointed minister of Chirnside, in Berwickshire.

Henry Erskine not only preached at his meeting house at Ravelaw (or Rivelaw, Revelaw or Reevelaw) but also at Newton (variously called Old Newton, Whitsome Newton and now East Newton) and at Whitsome Church;

the latter would have been the old church, nothing of which now remains, that stood in the centre of the churchyard and which was replaced by a new church in 1803. Henry Erskine inspired many others, including Thomas Boston of Ettrick, the Duns-born pastor and author of *Human Nature in its Fourfold State*.

There would have been no direct route between the hamlet of Ravelaw and the church and village of Whitsome and it would have been necessary to go west, south and then east by road. The one-inch to the mile Ordnance Survey map, First Edition, 1864, shows that the solution was a dog-legged track connecting the hamlet with the church and the village of Whitsome and the track is shown as crossing the small stone bridge. By 1897 when the Second Edition Ordnance Survey map was produced, the track had disappeared along with the hamlet. In the 17th century, if the Rev. Erskine was walking or riding to visit parishioners in Whitsome, the bridge could have been built to make his passage easier. It would also have benefited worshippers and other travellers from Ravelaw. For the writer, this unnamed and isolated bridge is, in its own modest way, another 'Bridge to Heaven'.

Bridges
by Heather Bolton

If on a panel game! I'd shout

"Bridges"- as all the clichés would emerge.

Clichés - so wonderful and right!

The intellectual chime

would be - "unproven this clichéd line."

"But who are you?" I'd say to them,

(scoffing all knowledge passed down to them!)

We do not know just why it's true

what Gran and HER mother said to you -

well known the trodden home truths are

they trip from tongue - so sweetly see....

"Don't burn your bridges" they'd shout at you!

Or in conventional office mode

you may be told "to bridge the gap"

where it is seen, a gap has widened –

an emergency, has opened up.

Or, perhaps it's someone with opposing views

who may have influence or skills

necessary to help the firm - diplomacy

may be the game with tolerance, and restraint.

Put into a greater broader scale it could

be multiplied to people - where gaps

yawn wide: ideologies clash

or perhaps its values - or the competition,

or disagreement between great states.
When fighting starts first target is the bridges -
destroy, divisive - division - a ploy:
difference, divide and burn the bridges,
leads one to say: again, "build more bridges!"
Not easy to build or to maintain, whether in mind
or with intent, but Scotland is proud,
to make great bridges. Across the Forth
even the Tay, so, how dare they say!
McGonagall was a rotten poet!
I have to say, until this day -
his poem lives on - with new bridge waiting
to cross the Tay.

The Bridge to *Xibalba*
by Oliver Eade

(Extract from 'Golden Jaguar of the Sun', first book of a YA cross-cultural trilogy, 'From Beast to God', that spans different dimensions.)

Adam Winters and his Mexican girlfriend, María, are on the run from drug gangsters in the Chiapas jungle of Mexico when the girl dies following a spider bite. Because of who she really is, of which the boy is unaware, she must be brought back to life. Adam travels with her to the Mayan Place of Fear, Xibalba, where all dead souls who have died naturally must first go. Here he will have to challenge the Great Spider Goddess to obtain spider venom with which to make an anti-venom that may prevent her death in a re-wind of her life in the world of the living. To get there, the teenagers cross a narrow suspension bridge that passes over a void also known as Hell...

*****

He halted at the edge of a bottomless chasm, from where Adam made out a towering arch – the beginning of a narrow suspension bridge, which disappeared into a swirling, grey mist. This was the bridge over which they would have to pass; the bridge to Xibalba, the 'Place of Fear' whence no dead soul is meant to return...

...Having bidden the Golden Jaguar farewell, Adam took María's hand and led her underneath the high archway and onto the bridge. Terror filled the girl's eyes. He sensed her trying to hold back and feared she already knew she was dead and that the place on the other side of this bridge was a land from which dead souls do not return.

"It's okay, María," Adam said softly, kissing her forehead. "You'll be fine. We're gonna win, the two of us. Remember? Carla and Pepe? The two children? *Our* children?"

Special? Was it Carla or Pepe who would turn out to be special? Were they what this was all about? Had María been chosen for something way beyond the understanding of the ancient gods?

An uneasy smile appeared on María's drawn face as they walked on into the mist. When Adam turned to look back, all he could see were the eyes of the Golden Jaguar. Ahead was a silent, grey void, and below, nothing. Adam held on to María whilst steadying himself with the handrail. The

10

bridge bounced with each step. To bounce on a narrow bridge spanning such a void should have sent the most intrepid of souls scuttling back to the safety of the edge of the chasm, but not Adam. He was resolute. He *would* save his girlfriend. They *would* have a life together.

Gently coaxing her forward, he slow-stepped his way towards *Xibalba*. When the other arch first appeared, silhouetted through the ghostly grey haze, Adam felt almost relieved that ahead was the place where he would perhaps get what was needed to give the girl back her life. As they inched forwards a dark shape appeared out of the mist: a motionless figure. Closer, he saw the figure was made of stone, but it was the face that caused Adam to turn round and cover María's eyes with his hand. A young man, frozen in fear during an obvious attempt to escape from *Xibalba*, his expression showed indescribable horror. Still shielding his girlfriend's eyes, and trying not to look at the nightmare image, Adam pushed past the man.

"Who *was* that?" asked the girl as they passed under the arch of the bridge and on to Xibalba.

"A statue," replied Adam. "Just a statue, María, and not a very good one. Rubbish compared with Rodin!"

The mist cleared, replaced by a fine, freezing drizzle. Ahead lay a vast and strange-looking land...

And returning from Xibalba across the bridge...

...Adam felt the girl's arm about his shoulder tighten as he sprinted onto the swing bridge. He knocked aside the frozen statue-man, causing it to shatter into a billion particles of shimmering death-dust and the dust merged with the bleak, dull-grey, misty drizzle. He ran on with María through the wet mist and shattered-soul dust and continued running whilst the bridge shook and bounced over that bottomless chasm: the chasm of a place known on earth as 'Hell', elsewhere as the ninth dimension. The arch at the other end of the bridge loomed out of the mist, becoming clearer all the time, and beyond that two bright points of fire penetrated the haze: the eyes of the Golden Jaguar.

Adam forced his legs to carry him and María at an athlete's pace under and beyond the arch and off the bridge. The Golden Jaguar, his eyes burning like white hot coals, bounded up to the steps leading down from the bridge. Still holding the girl, Adam straddled the beast's back and the Golden Jaguar shot forward, a godly arrow from an invisible bow, straight into the black gash scoring the dark mountain ahead.

?

by Jane Pearn

You would confront it but
it slinks round the corner
of the library smearing the windows with

words that leach from the bricks,
trail behind it like thick chattering smoke.

It stands below you in the shadow
of bridges (you cross each one as you come
to it). The waters are troubled.

It taps you on the shoulder.
Hot and urgent breath. Cunning,

you don't turn round but reach a hand back to
grab its coat which falls in flat
felted folds from your fingers

while it laughs hunched into a question
in the next street.

Interconnection
by Naomi Green

The tracks were always glistening at this time of the morning. She stepped over them on tiptoe, trying to avoid the grey, brittle stones between the slats of the old wooden sleepers. She knew you should never cross a railway line, but the bridge was out too far from her side of the station, and she was late for the train. As she crossed, she noticed some pure white flowers nestling in the gravel. Their quiet beauty shone out from the dark stones around them.

She climbed up the steep slope to the platform, and was arrested by the sight of a man walking along it. He seemed slightly agitated, yet purposeful, and his neat clothing did not suggest a man who might become easily perturbed. He was of average height, with bristling brown hair and dark, deep-set eyes. His general air and measure of step suggested the gait of an ex-soldier. She tried not to stare, but his identity seemed shielded and she thought that he might be foreign. Suddenly, she determined that somehow she would get him to speak to her, or at least be near enough to hear his accent. In her opinion, no person's identity was complete without that knowledge; voice was not just a part of somebody, but a reflection of their nation, culture and lifetime experience.

The guard's whistle sounded and she boarded the train, attempting to see where the man got on. She looked down the platform, and strangely, could see him engaged in some apparent argument with the guard. She strained to hear his voice, but could not. After a few seconds, the guard shot an aggressive gesture at the man and he quickly stepped aboard.

She got in and sat in her seat a few carriages away from this spectacle, and as she did, she felt an irresistible urge to walk down and talk to this mysterious gentleman, but restrained herself. She needed time to collect her thoughts, so sat down and took off her hat and gloves. She felt as if her inner life was inextricably linked to this foreign person who sat somewhere further up the 10.40 to York. She let her eyes rest and felt the warm sun playing on her eyelids. In a moment she was asleep, so imperceptibly, that she didn't have time to ask the person opposite to wake her at her station.

In a panic, she awoke and an inner voice seemed to be telling her it was too late, and that the man would have left the train by now. She opened her eyes and let her vision focus on the little old lady who had been seated opposite. But it was him.

This intriguing, foreign gentleman was sitting across from her, eyes alert, and searching her face, as if waiting for the answer to a question he had already asked. The sense of connection with him deepened and she responded to his look confidently, as if they already knew one another, and had been engaged in an intimate conversation. "You have slept deeply," he said and his voice fell over her like a brown mantle, liquid soft and definitely foreign.

"Yes," she said. She continued looking at him, internalising his strangeness and yet sudden familiarity. "You are a foreigner," she said, "Let me try and guess which country you are from." He smiled, and some of the agitation she had observed before fell away.

She looked at his face more closely. It was slightly lined around the eyes and mouth - he must laugh a lot, she thought, but also on the forehead, a suggestion of worry. A life lived deeply and energetically. His skin was olive-toned and his eyes were arched by quite bushy eyebrows. His lips were full and expressive and he was a little unshaven, though not in an unkempt fashion. He broke into a smile. "Well," he said, "have you guessed from where I originate?" A native English speaker would have used the words, 'guessed my country of origin.' His choice of words belied a certain level of understanding in English - familiar, but not yet fluent.

"Are you Russian?" she asked, somewhat coyly, expecting him to break into an intimidating laugh at her mistake.

"You are correct in a way," he replied. "My country used to belong to the Soviet Union, but no longer, since 1991."

"Oh, then you must come from somewhere like Ukraine?" She hesitated, trying to ascertain if her answer was correct by the tilt of his head.

"You have guessed it," he said, appraisingly, and she felt warmed by his response. It seemed suddenly reassuring after her initial determination to discover his true identity.

"How have you come to be seated here?" she asked, "I noticed you got on further up the train." And then wished she hadn't told him. He would know that her eyes had been following him.

"Yes," he said, "you are observant, and I also noticed that you saw my disagreement with the guard. I wanted to come and explain. You seem the right person to talk to."

So, the connection is there, she thought. Across landmasses, cultures, journeys, we meet and fall in with each other, like entering a plot that has taken over our lives.

"You seemed upset." She looked at him to see if his eyes might be etched with concern at her knowledge.

"I was," he said quietly, his voice lowered to the level of secrets and espionage.

"What is wrong?" she asked. She was aware that she had leant forward and was touching his hand. She drew back a little, wanting to enhance the distance between them again. Did she want this to be a part of her life, a thread in her tapestry that it might be difficult to remove?

Maybe it could just remain an excursion into a surreal world from which she could easily escape. She imagined herself recounting the story the next day to her friend in a cafe. They would laugh, and dismiss the whole incident with a slurp of their steaming hot coffee.

"I might be arrested at the next station," he whispered. "I only have a little time." He spoke in a matter of fact tone, as if he were telling her that he must hurry because of an appointment at the dentist.

"Arrested? Why?" She couldn't help sounding alarmed now. What had she got herself into? She noticed the cloud that had passed over his face. It looked ashen despite his calm voice.

"They think I am someone else," he said, "someone who was a spy in your British parliament during the communist years. The guard thought I was him too, but I just look like this man, I am not a spy. What can I do?" He had become more and more agitated during this explanation until his last words became a helpless appeal to her. She felt horror-stricken. Here she was on a typical train journey, and had gone from being intrigued by the look and step of a man to being involved with the very sinews of his life.

She made her choice and gave him a reassuring smile. "That is my stop too," she said. "I'll get off with you and we'll face it together."

He took her hand warmly. "I knew I could trust you." He searched her eyes and found the surety that he needed in the return of her steady gaze.

At the next stop, they got off. It was a small country station, virtually deserted. The autumn sun was shining on the tracks, making them look mellow and golden. Two men came out of the old station house, one official-looking in a well-cut business suit, the other a policeman. The first man strode up purposefully. "Mr Sarokorpov?"

"Yes?" the Ukrainian replied in a firm voice. He seemed calmer now, resigned to his fate.

"You are a free man," responded the official, suddenly taking his hand and shaking it heartily. "We found the imposter who framed you, and we are dreadfully sorry for our mistake." Mr Sarokorpov looked wildly and delightedly into the eyes of his new and trusted friend. "Can I take you out for a meal?" he asked.

And suddenly
by Robert Leach

And suddenly there it was –

    Smoothed by many feet, nail heads

    Rusty brown, mere pecks

    In worn grey boards, their ends

    Borne up by metal handrails: the whole

    Hammocked in sweeping curves of metal ropes

    Slung from sentinel end-towers.

    Below – a deft tinkling of unending flow. Then

    A small sniff of autumn

    In the drifts of breeze,

    A sweet rottenness, decay,

    And a touch too much

    Of swaying, swaying

    To show how time touched base.

    An exercise in perspective,

    The way foreshortened,

    Yet never quite

    Dwindled to a point, a speck,

    A mere mote, and lost.

And so we crossed.

Somewhere Across The Universe
by Keith Farnish

I can't see through the window just now because I'm staring at the wall. On the other side of it, but far, far away, is my Dad.

We had an argument. This is normal, we argue a lot, but this time something broke. There's no point shouting or going out looking because I don't think he's coming back. So I'm staying here, my pyjamas lit by the streetlights, bare feet speckled by the tops of the shrubs I was meant to help him tidy up.

There was a moment in the morning, half way through my first cup of tea and a quarter of the way through jam on toast, that we connected. But just for a moment. I smiled, he smiled. Then the radio told of some party leader who wasn't getting the support of his MPs, and his face turned down, as though it mattered. I finished my toast, my tea, and put the crocks in the washing up bowl. Dad carried on listening to the radio, because it mattered.

I offered to help with the kitchen after a while, but he was managing fine without me, thank you very much. Sarcasm.

Saturdays don't feel like the start of the weekend, but Sundays feel like the end, like it's winding down and getting you all ready for school when you have to empty your bag, find your uniform, check your timetable, do any homework you forgot to finish. Prepare for the week ahead. I can't enjoy Saturdays because I know the next day is Sunday and that's when the weekend finishes. But I try my best.

He calls to me later on, says I should wear scruffy clothes, not my pyjamas, and have I brushed my teeth yet? I haven't, it's Saturday, my teeth can rot for a few hours more. Pyjamas are so comfortable, anyway. Why are daytime clothes all stiff and starchy with sharp edges? Maybe it's to keep us awake when we secretly want to be in our pyjamas and feeling sleepy again. Even jeans don't feel that comfortable, and they're called 'comfortable clothes'. I'm not getting changed yet, even though I can hear the sound of the shed door being unlocked.

It was lunch by the time he came upstairs. Outside, through the gap between my curtains, I had watched him, moving slowly, looking small in the middle of the lawn, dragging the mower before pushing it forwards again. He had stopped bothering with stripes a long time ago; stopped pulling up the daisies and the dandelions which keep spreading as he forgets to mow.

He never used to forget to mow, but that was before.

I pulled the curtains tight, so didn't see if he looked up. He knew I was there, because I hadn't gone down to help with the tools or the wheelbarrow or cutting down the shrubs Mum had kept so carefully pruned when she was around. He wanted to make them neat, for her, and had asked me to help, for her. For him as well.

The front door opens, then closes and sucks air from the house. He'll be taking off his gardening shoes so no grass gets onto the carpet, and definitely no mud. That wouldn't be right. The stairs creak a little and there's an odd double bump as his feet go down on the third and fourth stair and lift up again. I don't know what makes that bump; I stood on those stairs for hours, lifting my feet up and putting them down again, trying to work out how, if the stairs moved then they didn't fall right down to the bottom of the house. But he's past those stairs and almost at the top. His footsteps are so different to those of Mum. I used to hear them come to bed, lying under my duvet trying so hard to sleep.

There's a knock on the door. He wants to come in, wants to talk, again.

He knocks again and the door opens. I shout at him, swearing, don't come in MY ROOM, it's MY SPACE, my PRIVATE space. I'm wearing pyjamas, there's nothing to see, but it's still my room.

We don't talk, he says.

I don't want to talk.

We don't do anything together, he says.

Leave me alone.

His face is stretched and grey, I want to feel sorry for him, so sad, for Mum. What about me, though? Do you care how I feel?

Of course I care about you, more than anything.

Bring her back.

…

I can't.

Then get out.

He went and something broke.

Now he's on the other side of the wall, but he could be anywhere. I can't hear any bumps, any tools, any water running or dishes being washed. I can't hear him breathe. Somewhere across the universe, he's there waiting for me. Just waiting, but I'm in my pyjamas in my private space, with the street lamp shining on me and the wall, and my feet with speckles moving as the shadows of the leaves of the shrubs Mum used to keep so tidy move in the wind.

He won't hear me.

...

I can't reach the top of the shrubs, but I don't want to cut too low. I don't want to cut in the wrong place in the dim light, or hurt my fingers when I slip, though who would care if I did? Then I feel him near, his breath in my hair, his fingers taking the secateurs from out of my hand and reaching higher so he can cut just above the newly emerging buds.

Then he gives them back to me and I look down at what he has brought out. I stand on the step, turn around, put my arms around him and hold tight.

Causeway
by Laurna Robertson

So much sky, so much sea,
so little land and every pool
filled with blue.

The tide unzips from the causeway,
cord grass and meadow sedge
flex back from its grasp.

Cars leave tyre tracks on the wet road.
Keels of tarred boats are black fins
circling on waves of whin grass.

Oyster-catchers skirt the sand dunes.
Winds whistle through lobster pots,
over coiled rope and bluster round me

asking why I have come.

Don't Burn Your Bridges
by Raghu Shukla

Bridges, bridges, bridges. Bridges are everywhere. There are big bridges, from the Golden Gate Bridge to Sydney Harbour Bridge. And then there are smaller bridges scattered all over the world, just as useful.

This article, though, describes bridges, which can't be seen – but can be easily felt. They serve as emotional bonds and can be built anywhere and everywhere: in all walks of life, in all ages and all over the world. Happily, they are also the bricks of our daily lives. I am, of course, talking about 'bridges' metaphorically as well as in their expanded sense: to link, to mend, to connect, to unite, to reconcile, to make things smooth and to fill gaps or differences. Besides, the word has a positive and convivial connotation. All the reason then to be involved in building bridges. The positive (as well as hopefully-positive) outcome is discussed through the prism of personal experiences, three momentous events of 2016 (Brexit, the US Presidential Election and Syria) and international events.

Personal Experiences

I arrived in England (in 1969) with the two aims of working as a Consultant Physician in the NHS and travelling widely. After filling all the necessary criteria for the Consultant post, I met with a worldly professor to seek his general advice and guidance. The professor listened to me carefully and then uttered the magic word: bridges. "Let me explain what I mean," he said. "It's very difficult to get a Consultant job." And he went on, "but to secure your assignment, you need to build several bridges. All this will require time and patience." Without going into needless detail, suffice it to say I followed his recommendations to the letter and hey presto! I was appointed a Consultant in due course. Magic.

One success leads to another. It had been my ambition for some time to write/edit a book on the comprehensive care of elderly people – my domain. But how to go about it? My job provided me ample opportunity to travel globally and to attend medical conferences, from the USA to Australia. While visiting various cities – New York, Boston, Adelaide, Geneva, to name a few – I used the professor's mantra to liaise with several Consultant colleagues regarding their contributions to the book.

The outcome, after seven years of hard work, was welcoming. In 1996, my internationally contributed book was published. The book has been a source of joy ever since, more so after earning plaudits from hospital as well as General Practitioner colleagues from up and down the country.

National and International Perspectives

Brexit, the US Presidential election and the ongoing suffering in Syria are three pivotal events of the year. And, even though we have heard about them ad nauseam, there is no escaping from their consequential import.

Brexit

As we know, our decision to leave the EU following the June 2016 European Referendum was unexpected. It's a big worry for all of us and, of course, a gargantuan challenge for the government. But it has provided an opportunity too.

So, what are the challenges? The Brexit changeover is expected to be protracted and complex – a multi-faceted process. Although we are going to leave the EU (but not Europe), our friendly relationship is going to continue with European countries in important areas such as finance, security and many other fields. Also, the Brexit handover is two-way traffic: while we maintain a friendly relationship with the EU, we also expect a similar 'smooth' understanding from the European Union during the entire period of negotiations. After all, the Euro zone's financial stability is dependent on the City of London, which happens to be the crucial financial centre.

And the opportunity? Hopefully, both during and after the completion of the Brexit negotiations, we will be free to have trade-links with the wider world – USA, Australia, India and China, to name a few. A start has already been made: the recent visit to India by Prime Minister May is the first step in that direction. All in all, it's now time to go global. Of course, many more bridges will need to be built, to mutual benefit, across the world.

US Presidential Election

The 2016 US Presidential election was bitter, divisive and theatrical. In the past – I have seen at least ten of them – the campaigns have been dignified, smooth and a sort of beacon or 'bridge' for the rest of the world. This year's campaign, however, was anything but. The world is still experiencing the aftershocks of the election. Of course, both candidates, Hillary Clinton and Donald Trump, were trying to build bridges with the voters, but their modus operandi was quite different: whereas Clinton's play cards showed 'BUILD BRIDGES NOT WALLS' (an obvious reference to building a wall at the US/Mexican border), Mr Trump's slogan was 'MAKE AMERCA GREAT AGAIN' – rather melodramatic and in show-business style. Now that Mr Trump is the winner, it remains to be seen whether he goes ahead with his wall-building plan. Hillary Clinton's defeat does not in any sense reduce the core value of her 'bridging' campaign slogan.

It's worth pointing out that Mr Trump, to a large extent, was the beneficiary of his appearance in the American 'Apprentice' show several years ago. He became a national 'hero' after his appearance in the show, thus raising his public profile immensely. The 'bridge' he thus made, provided him, almost certainly, this Presidential gift. In spite of what we have all seen on TV or heard about Mr Trump, it's too early to pronounce any verdict on him. Who knows, he may turn out to be a charitable president by making bridges both at home and abroad. Human nature is not a fixed entity. Attitudes do change: time is the final arbiter.

Syria

What a crying shame. Syria does need a strong 'bridge' from the international community but, sadly, it's not forthcoming. What's so frustrating is that the various elements have been allowed to continue such unbearable atrocities for so long. Even the United Nations seems to be helpless to stop it.

Globalisation and Bridge-Making

We live in a global village. Globalisation is a strong 'bridge' between different countries of the world. It is powered by money, expertise and the workforce. In effect, it's due to the influence of large multinational companies – Google, Amazon, Uber and a few others in the field – and their efforts for technological advances. These advances, as we know, are the 'engines' of today's blissful life. Two decades ago, it took months to collect, say, 50,000 petitions for a cause. Today, thanks to social media, those petitions could be gathered within a week. But too much of a good thing may have a deleterious effect on society and it appears that we have now approached that state with globalisation: apart from corporate greed, there is the creation of social inequality. And social media (Twitter, for example) is being used for spats and even abuses in some cases, and by extremists for promoting their cause. Such side-effects of globalisation are clearly anything but bridge-building.

International Events and 'Bridges'

For years, international forums, conventions and competition events have been building strong bridges in various fields: social, arts, politics, finance etc. This is achieved not only by the exchange of novel ideas but by utilising the occasion to build personal bonds. The yearly jamboree – The World Economic Forum – at Davos in Switzerland is a shining example. The convention is attended by the good and the great from every corner of the world and from every organisation – industrialists, politicians (yes, our Prime Minister too), celebrities, economists and the CEOs of multinational companies. Other important events include G8/G20 meetings, The Cannes Film Festival, Book Festivals (Edinburgh and Frankfurt), musical events and, of course, the Olympic gathering every four years. All in all, the huge benefits of bridge-building can't be espoused enough.

What else? Two issues are worthy of mention.

Communications

An explicit and honest communication between two people underpins a lasting friendship. This is true for building bridges too. It's essential in any discussion: from management to workers; doctors to patients; politicians to their constituents and so on. Needless to say, many problems stem from ambiguous statements and misinformation.

The Social Mobility Problem

The greatest bane of our times is the problem of the widening gap in social mobility: the huge chasm that exists between the rich and the poor. This is seen across the board – not only in the major economies (in the UK itself, nearly 25 per cent of the national wealth is owned by just the upper one per cent) but also in emerging countries like India, China and Brazil for example. The all-too familiar mantra used by politicians, especially before elections, has sadly failed to bridge the gap between haves and have-nots. What's really needed is action, not only words.

So, there we have it. As a country in today's volatile world – particularly with the spectres of Brexit and Trump looming large - there is an urgent need for making bridges at all levels – political, economic, social and other fronts. To paraphrase Abraham Lincoln: destroy your enemies by making them your friends. Indeed. The best way to hold happiness in the palm of your hand is to build bridges and not to burn them, whenever and wherever it's possible. Equally, don't readily cross off 'old' and established friends from your Christmas card list!

I keep my Dearest next to me
by Heather Bolton

I keep my dearest

next to me

not displayed for

the world to see!

In my bedroom

near my bed –

you are not winning

a sport's event –

or are being given

your degree –

it is just

that you are dear

to me,

whatever

the event may be!

What about Tom?

by Margaret Skea

As the car reached the brow of the hill Claire swung it into the layby and cut the engine. Getting out she leant her elbows on the rough wall and stared at the old familiar landscape. It hadn't been a conscious decision to stop, rather the instinctive re-awakening of an old habit. A sign that she was home.

The valley lay before her like a crumpled patchwork quilt, a kaleidoscope of colour. From above, the hedges were low and irregular, outlining the pattern of fields, green and brown and flamboyant splashes of yellow rape. Later would come the pale creams and golds of early ripening corn and the blue linseed flower, later still the rich red of newly turned soil and the zebra-stripes of burnt stubble. Today, however, it was mid-May, the sun pale, the air damp and everywhere the distinctive sweet smell of the rape.

One by one she focused on the well-remembered features of the landscape: the thorn trees late in blossom, the old quarry cleft on the opposite hillside, the river which wound like a threaded ribbon through the fields and coverts, and the bridge, which stood, ancient and intriguing, linking nowhere with nowhere. All her life it had been the focal point of her 'once-upon-a-times'. In her imagination she had linked castle with abbey, granary with mill, manor with farm, Odysseus with Penelope...

He was there now, leaning on the parapet, looking up towards the road, looking directly at her. She narrowed her eyes against the sunlight. What was it made her so sure? Something in the angle of the head perhaps, the tilt of his cap, the taut stillness which communicated itself to her even across this distance. Behind him the ground rose towards a coppice, polka-dot sheep grazing on the spring-green grass. For a moment she stared downwards, aware of her own quickened breathing and the pain in her palms as her nails bit into the flesh. The ground was soft underfoot and the grass brushed across her ankles trailing dampness, which seeped through her tights and canvas pumps, chilling her feet. She walked steadily, refusing to give in to her desire to hurry, refusing to admit, even to herself, the old feelings, which stirred within her.

It had all been so long ago. She had made her choice and it had been the right one. She had been sure of that. And though she enjoyed the infrequent family get-togethers and the seasonal junketing with old friends, she had always returned to her wider world with a sense of relief, less safe perhaps, but less constricting.

Now as she picked her way towards the bridge she felt, for the first time, confused. It would take no more than five minutes. Five minutes to conquer the butterflies in her stomach, the racing of her pulse, the rush of saliva in her mouth. Five minutes to regain her composure, to suppress the unruly thoughts, which slipped unbidden into her mind. She had come this way so often before and little had changed. The rickety wooden stile between Long Meadow and the Half-Acre, the rooks cawing high above the ring of pines, the untidy jumble of stones in the stream-bed, the trickle of water, peat-brown.

She was close enough now to see the way his hair curled untidily on his collar, the small tear at the corner of his jacket pocket, and the slight shine at the knees of his corduroys. "Hello, Tom." Her voice was as cool as she could make it.

"Claire... you weren't expected." It was a statement, not a question.

For the first time she understood why he had never been around when she visited. He must have been forewarned and so had stayed away.

"They don't know I'm here. It's just ... I need to talk things over with Mum and Dad." The silence stretched between them, difficult, uncomfortable. High up the valley a tractor coughed into life, spluttered, then died again.

Tom looked at his watch. His voice was diffident, careful. "If you're not expected ... we could have lunch ... I usually cook enough for two days running. His grin was still boyish. "If you care to risk it and," with a glance at his wellingtons, "If you don't mind mud in your car."

As they pulled up in the farmhouse yard, Claire thought, 'Nothing has changed.'

But sitting at the table enjoying a surprisingly good lunch, she changed her mind. At first conversation was awkward. Tom talked about the farm, sheep prices, the Common Agricultural Policy and Brexit, and Claire felt a world away from it all. He asked about her work. At first she was hesitant, then the words began to spill out, filling the spaces between them. The London office, the view over Tower Bridge, a job she loved, and now, the opportunity to go to Sydney. The challenge, the excitement ... her hesitation. "It's so far away. So final."

*

At home, Claire explained to her parents. "I need to tell them by Friday."

Her mother was brisk and practical. "A golden opportunity. Don't let it slip."

Her father was encouraging and sympathetic. "We could come for Christmas, beat the cold." Only her sister, in the quietness of the room they'd shared as children, dared to ask, "What about Tom?"

"What about Tom? It was a question that she birled around in her mind until she was almost dizzy with the thought of it. As a child he had been the pivotal point in her world. As a teenager marriage to Tom, life with Tom had seemed the inevitable conclusion to their childhood friendship. But then had come college and Claire's first glimpse of a world in which he had no part. She had grown up and away and had thought herself gone for good. But now, she realized, the valley and Tom had always been there, in the background, a kind of safety net, an option not quite closed. But Sydney...

Over the next few days she tramped up and down the valley, revisiting old haunts, seeing her home from every vantage point, filling her mind with a gallery of pictures to treasure. She revelled in the lush, green dampness, the early morning cool, the light evening breezes which fanned her face and lifted her hair. Memories were everywhere. And in an endless cycle her decision came back to one single question. 'What about Tom?' She didn't know.

Standing on the bridge, running her fingers backwards and forwards over the rough stone and picking at the lichens that clung tenaciously to the crevices between the blocks, she thought, 'My life is punctuated by bridges. This one, my past, Tower Bridge my present, the future? This one ... or ... In her mind's eye she saw the soaring arcs of Sydney Opera House and the clean, clear lines of the bridge that spanned the harbour. From her office she would be able to watch the sun dimpling the water and the constant movement of traffic backwards and forwards over the bridge. If she went.

*

The office block rose out of a smother of trees. Claire sat, staring out through the huge picture-window. In the distance the Blue Mountains were a low smudge on the horizon and on the south shore the office towers glittered, Manhattan-like. Below her the water was an impressionist stipple: green, white, silver. Dark silhouettes of sleek yachts, their tall masts needle-thin, dipped and swayed in the early morning breeze. The first ferry ploughed across the bay.

She hadn't tried to describe it, for it defied description. She had simply written Claire on the back of the card and sent it off. She remembered his last words, as they stood together leaning on the parapet of the bridge, elbows touching.

"Send me a postcard ... of *your* bridge. Maybe..." he had smiled sideways at her, a crooked, half-smile, "There are a lot of sheep in Australia."

Scott's Bridge to Rhymer's Glen
by Anita John

I search for where it might have been,
deep in the glen among tall sitka spruce,
and find two wooden beams or fallen trees –
moss coated, lichen stitched –
crossing from one side to the other.
I would trust my weight to their strength
in this green and eldritch licht
but I am neither child nor fairy-light.

Onwards then to Bowden Moor
with a growing sense of watching.
The moor shrouds itself in a close-dressed haar
and the silver threads of spiders' webs
catch and throw the light so everything shimmers
in obliterating brightness.
All sound hushed save for the fragile chink
of a single bird in an unseen tree.

I've stepped, it seems, into a place
where truth and myth have merged as one.
Then the sun insists on burning off the fret
and my vision of Scott's Rhymer's Glen is gone.

The Chinese Bridge
by Pamela Gordon Hoad

The man stood at the French windows, his back to the thing behind him, and he stared out at the terraces leading down to the loch. He glimpsed his reflection in the glass and straightened his powdered wig. Then he pulled down his waistcoat and brushed his breeches with his hand, smoothing the creases where he had knelt. It would not do to let the servants see him with a less than immaculate appearance. Emotions must be kept behind closed doors and shut mouths, suppressed so effectively that they gave no discernible hint of distress.

The view always gave him satisfaction and a sense of continuity, in spite of everything. His grandfather had been responsible for planting the avenue of trees from the gates to the front of the house in the 1750s and his father had erected the classical façade to disguise the older building inside this shell. His father had also imposed symmetry on the natural water feature so that the banks curved round the sides of the ornamental loch with pleasing regularity. His own contribution to improving his inheritance was mainly directed to the wider estate, enclosing fields and introducing flocks of Cheviot sheep from Northumberland to nibble the grass where once ramshackle shacks and byres obtruded on the orderly landscape. It had been necessary to relocate the human occupants but he prided himself that he had acted fairly, providing decent new cottages out of sight of the house, and he deprecated the actions of landowners who turned their tenants off the land with arbitrary abandon. It pleased him to be an exemplary laird.

In making his improvements he had indulged in one flight of fancy, one venture into the picturesque which had become so popular among people of refined taste who dotted their woodlands with Grecian temples and ready-made ruined follies. He had surveyed the outlook from the house and decided it lacked a focus which would give distinction and perhaps a delightful quaintness to the panorama. He had discussed this conclusion with a garden designer, one of the best in the country, and as a result he introduced the Chinese bridge at the far end of the loch where the ground was marshy. He had surrounded it with tastefully rugged rocks and well-chosen wild vegetation and he had the bottom of the loch dredged so there was a depth of water to catch the reflection of this exquisite artifice on a bright day. The bridge had no practical purpose whatever as it was perfectly possible to walk round the end of the loch only twenty yards beyond the structure but practicality was not the point.

From the window he gazed at the bridge, gleaming in the rays of the setting sun, and studied the broad latticework along its sides with its angular, fretwork pattern. He had it constructed for Miranda, in the weeks before their marriage when he was anxious to provide an appropriate setting for his incomparable bride, a hot-house bloom nurtured in the fashionable salons of Edinburgh and plucked from that rarefied world to grace his Borders backwater. Chinoiserie was all the rage, he was told. Wallpaper with miniature pagodas and ladies in kimonos carrying parasols decorated the walls of most grand houses but he had decided to go one better, to create an actual Chinese feature, integral to the scenery they would see from the principal windows. He had never been sure that she appreciated his installation with the intensity he hoped for but she had humoured him, praising the appearance of the bridge and the interest it gave to the otherwise rather nondescript end of the loch. She had even consented to walk down to it and lean on its balustrade, with the lace at her wrist fluttering in the breeze, while the unparalleled Henry Raeburn sketched her likeness. Back in his studio the artist had produced a charming portrait which now graced the main stairway of the house and caught the eye of every visitor. Nevertheless her husband thought it did not do her justice as that disdainful tilt of her chin was not her most notable characteristic and her expression in the picture might be considered morose rather than thoughtful.

He treasured the portrait now despite its flaws for it was all he had to help him recall her beauty and whenever he looked at it the pain of losing her was renewed. Everyone knew childbirth was a risky business and Miranda was delicate in build but his own mother was tiny and she had borne ten children, outliving all but three. He had engaged the most renowned midwife in the district to supervise his wife's lying-in and care for her recovery but it was not to be. The Minister counselled him to take comfort in the fact that he had experienced nearly three years of joyful union with this paragon and to be grateful for the gift heaven had vouchsafed him. 'The Lord giveth and the Lord taketh away' was a prudent man's mantra. He did not find this as consoling as a virtuous man should and held himself blameworthy.

The gift actually vouchsafed him had been Kitty who nestled on her mother's breast for four days before Miranda succumbed to the fever. Kitty became the centre of his life from then on, his hope to see the image of his wife created anew, his promise of future joy in watching the child grow to womanhood. She was an adorable baby – how could she be otherwise? Topped by fair curls which bobbed with her every move, lively and inquisitive, she was admired throughout the neighbourhood. Yet her father felt inadequate during her infancy while nursemaids had charge of her for he could hardly indulge in the childish behaviour they adopted when amusing her. He remained a distant and austere figure on the threshold of the nursery, surveying the winsome child with delight but failing to engage her attention. He persuaded himself he must be patient until she grew in intelligence and he could talk to her as to an adult woman of reasonable, albeit inevitably limited, ability about the pursuits which interested him.

He acknowledged privately that he should have remarried. Three years was too long to leave the little girl without a female guardian to teach her feminine graces and replicate a mother's love. Even the most superior servants offered no substitute for a lady of quality beside the cradle and, when the time came to employ a governess, her function would be instruction not cherishment. He had not realised soon enough how irresponsible he was, how neglectful of his duty, but he had prized the memory of Miranda's presence and felt no inclination, on his own account, to accept a replacement by his hearth. He had been negligent in not appreciating that Kitty needed a mother, that a multitude of caring attendants could never fill the place Miranda had left empty.

He leaned his forehead against the pane of glass and stifled the instinct to sob. Then he turned with deliberate slowness and walked back across the room to the diminutive catafalque where his daughter's body rested. He looked down on her unnaturally placid face and twined his finger in a wayward curl. They had cleaned the mud from her features but he observed a speck caught on her hairline and gently he removed it. There was a graze on her cheek and he supposed she must have scraped it on a twig or stone when she fell. Her mouth was slightly open, as if rebuking him for all time. From the neck down she was swaddled in grave clothes, confining those previously active limbs in eternal stillness. Her appearance was an affront to nature, a reproach to the father who had betrayed her trust.

He turned away, consumed with fury, punching his fist onto a table. The Chinese bridge must be destroyed. He would have it demolished in the morning, each plank shattered and burned, the plants around it uprooted, the rocks smashed. It was a thing malignant in its conception. The gaps between the decorative slats were too wide. Could the designer not see that a small child might clamber through and fall? Surely the man was culpable? They said her heavy dress would have dragged her under the water and she must have caught her foot in the undergrowth so she could not struggle free. Her plunge had churned up sludge at the bottom of the loch, clogging her mouth and nose with mire; if she had screamed her cry might have been smothered and therefore went unheard.

He stood by the window once more, clutching its frame with taut fingers, shaking with knowledge of the truth. He would never attempt to pin blame on the designer for fear questions would be asked and the circumstances of the accident probed. As it was, no one would do more than shake their heads and mutter 'reprehensible neglect', 'disgraceful negligence', 'appalling dereliction', without thought of pursuing retribution which could not restore the lost child to life. What rightly should be done had been done. The nursemaid had been dismissed immediately, ejected from the house that same day, sent off without a reference, discredited and condemned: the nursemaid who should have accompanied the child step by step beside the loch, controlling her instinct for adventure, preventing her from venturing onto the tantalising bridge, seizing her skirts if she had disobeyed. The wretched young woman had bowed her head in contrition, her cheeks aflame with shame for her inattentiveness, but she had accepted the payment he had given her to keep her mouth shut.

Several times in the past few weeks he had contrived to encounter Maisie as she walked with Kitty in the grounds and, when they were screened by the bushes, she had let him fondle her while the child chased the blowing leaves or rolled on the grassy slopes. Five days ago he had raised Maisie's skirt and whispered pernicious endearments but the gardeners were nearby and might have intruded on their shady dell so he went no further. He knew Maisie was flattered and excited by her master's attentions. He knew also she was an honest, inexperienced girl who might well entertain some dream of preferment at his side, perhaps fostered by romantic tales the servants gleaned from sensational newssheets. She had agreed to meet him again, by intent, in a more secluded place, not far from the Chinese bridge, where they were confident Kitty would be happy, scrambling by a shallow pool, looking for tiddlers and building tiny dams with stones by the waterside. The location had fulfilled all his expectations, giving them seclusion, and Maisie had proved delightfully compliant. They did not notice that Kitty had run off from the spot where they had left her, to climb onto the shiny baluster of the bridge and squeeze between its too-wide struts. They did not even hear her cry of alarm when she tumbled through the gap and plopped into the water, dampening the overhanging branches with spray from her fatal baptism in the loch.

That was her father's secret ignominy with which he must live forever, the understanding that he was in effect the murderer of his own child, of Miranda's child. Brief, thoughtless gratification had destroyed all she had left him and the sight of the Chinese bridge taunted him with his lethal irresponsibility. In a dreadful shattering of his self-control, he banged his head on the windowpane, tore off his wig and gave the roar of an anguished animal pierced to the heart. The sound echoed through the silent house and, in blank misery, he did not care who heard him.

Not just any day in the life
by Toni Parks

Mundane daily routine
Wifely duties mount so
Clock watching ever slo-mo
Nothing to excite

Be careful what you wish for
Shake off languid stupor
Grass may not be greener on
the riverbank's other side

Consider that a burnt bridge
takes longer in the rebuild
So keep all options open
live life here and now

Unexpecteds lurk to
thwart a mapped out future
Readings on a palm raised
stifling the unstoppable
scr..e…a….m

Bridges seduced by burns
by Bridget Khursheed

Come with me, forget your fingers of mere

reeds and whitethroats -

whole grass seed peace -

the muir fall of autumn.

Don't you want to see

the tidefast end of it all;

stanchions stabbing the water in

the battle of tide, crusted shell and freshet?

This is your migration.

Why always be the one returned to?

Your aching boards only a recipient

of fox pad and mustelid scrape -

that pontoon pause - come

feel even your structural bricks, all neat and tight,

shuck away like pearled eyes,

stream deep into my gunshot flood.

Reflections on Bridges
by Gillian Vickers

I don't like bridges, at least big metal ones. I find heavy, geometric metallic constructions that do not follow the colours and contours of nature ugly. Give me a pale blue shimmering lake or a snow-capped mountain any day rather than the San Francisco Bridge or the Eiffel Tower. For me there is no comparison in terms of beauty. Regardless of how clever the designs are I see metal bridges as scars on the landscape. The only bridges that appeal to me are old stone ones that don't stand out like sore thumbs, like little moss-covered ones that nestle discretely among the Fells in the Lake District and merge with the countryside. Or tiny bridges that cross the complex waterways in Venice that look like part of the adjacent buildings and surrounding landscape.

I have never enjoyed crossing big bridges. I find other means of crossing water like beautiful yachts, ferries or rowing boats prettier and much more romantic. I would not go as far as to say I have a phobia of bridges but as soon as I realise that I am on one I start to feel apprehensive and think about its age and construction. Has it been adequately maintained over the years? Was it built for all this heavy traffic? Are the foundations sound? Then, if I am driving, I worry that I am distracted and looking around instead of focusing on the road. I grit my teeth, face forward, keep a steady pace and am relieved when I reach the other side.

I know that my feelings are out of proportion to the risks involved. Statistics tell me that I am more likely to die crossing the road, flying in a plane or even being hit by the proverbial bus! However, my fear remains, which I suppose dates back to my childhood. Growing up in Edinburgh in the 1960s and 70s I was constantly made aware of the dangers of the Forth Road Bridge, which as a small child seemed like a monster on the edge of the city. The news on the TV and radio regularly reported accidents on the bridge, people committing suicide by jumping off it as well as warnings and closures due to 'severe weather'. Scenes of the formidable construction being battered by the wind and rain as cars and lorries struggled to cross it were etched on my memory at an early age.

On the rare occasions that we crossed the Forth Road Bridge, heading north for a family holiday in Perthshire, I was filled with excitement and trepidation as we approached the monster. The fact that we had to pay to cross it added to the drama and it suddenly became a ride in a theme park. The cars and lorries slowed down as they approached the bridge and formed multiple queues at the tollbooths. We joined the shortest one and my Dad fumbled in his pockets and my Mum in her purse looking for change. I looked at the man in the booth and thought that must be the most boring job in the world.

As we crossed the bridge it juddered and swayed and I was convinced that something was wrong. I looked out at the water below, a long way down and imagined us falling into it. I looked up at the girders and the men painting them and again thought, what a horrible job. Finally the last bump came, back onto terra firma, a smooth road ahead and we entered The Kingdom of Fife. I felt safe again and did not need to worry about bridges... at least until Perth!

Selkirk Bridge
by Tom Murray

Birthed in a rage of Ettrick Water
my broad muscled back carries the strain
amid monozygotic town and country.
Built to purpose I do not complain.

'81 the year of my abrupt birth.
I have no history to speak of.
Building my own, scavenging rubble
of my tragic ancestors' downfall.

Boots bloodied in victory and defeat.
Bleating befuddled shepherded sheep.
Cows heavy hoofed to market.
Eventually something had to give.

'77 the year Old Stane Brig's death.
Caught unawares by his erstwhile friend
complacent of its dormant strength.

Ettrick Water sozzled on cocktails
of wind and rain clung to him, buckled
limbs, ancient heart crashed overwhelmed.

Guilt haunts me at the thought of it.

Must last the centuries as tribute.

No distinction amid town and country.

A neutral conduit of give and take.

The Faces of Bridge Therapus
by Hayley M. Emberey

When the sun rises in the east, the silhouetted border of Chiminga Valley becomes drowned, the shape rapidly erased by rippled sheets of golden, white light. The piercing eruption of breathtaking luminosity awakens Rico McTyde, Demigod of the Fifth Haven Upper Realm, even more so than usual since it is the morning of a New Moon. The sky has to be completely crystal clear, cloudless; to stir Rico McTyde from the depths of his immortal slumbering state, the sky a blank canvas on which the sun can flick specks of brushed white, orange and golden yellow. It is Sunday 27th January 2045, the day of the Wolf Moon, the first of the eleven annual moons. The compelling glow of the Wolf Moon's preceding sun is so commanding, a moaning groan is unleashed from the twenty-year old Rico as he rolls to one side. Placing the back of one of his hands over his eyes, his bent arm moves for the first time in a while, his face and figure swerve in the direction of his bedroom window. Eyes scrunched, barely open, the twenty year old reaches for his retro sunglasses, his pupils breathing a sigh of relief once shielded. There is little point in wrestling with the force of the beaming sun, for it is ancient, the breath of all life, the source of planet Earth's entire existence and survival.

Rico has always followed the sun's presence since he was a small child. His grandfather, Molecular McTyde, ancient Zen Master and Prophet of the Third Haven Upper Realm, advised him to do so one morning when they sat reading about 'Adaheli', the sun-god in Surinam Indian myth. For twenty years, Rico had watched humans or Earthlings as they were sometimes known to Demigods, attempting, some with more success than others, to link to the moon cycles; to follow the constellations; to work with the ancient mountains or the deepest secrets of the oceanic underworld. This morning, the Earth's sun had something to show Rico that would challenge his status again, his grandfather had premonisced this memorable day fifteen years ago, the year he was killed.

Lying motionless, the old, oak bedroom door creaked slowly open, the delicate sound of what seemed like wooden hooves tapping on its beams. In walked Rico's sister Disir, minor goddess of The Fifth Haven Upper Realm and her childhood friend, Clytie, nymphette also of The Fifth Haven Upper Realm. Both were bursting with excitable and uncontrollable, zestful energy. They weren't usually up at this time but they felt the stirring presence of illumination penetrating through all the walls of the house. Rico shuffled across the crisp, blue bed sheets, the warm space now vacant to accommodate both girls to sit and observe. The bedroom smelled of scented beeswax candles, a damp bathroom towel and Diet Coke. A humming silence endured, bright light bore through the window painting sharp rectangles on the lush carpet. Particles of dust danced lazily in the beams of sunlight cascading into the bedroom and all three of our immortal subjects found themselves with their heads stuck rigid in awe staring out of the window.

"What in Beetles' name are those?" Rico whispered tentatively, pointing at unusually shaped images sitting in the centre of the sun, formations which his eyes hadn't yet witnessed despite all the hours spent in the presence of the sun, studying it, following it, loving it and bathing in its warmth and glory. Disir and Clytie scuffled in closer to observe by what it was Rico was so entranced. With the absence of a filter to hide their eyes from the light, it was impossible to see anything with such a blinding strength, so the girls had to run out and seek some form of eye protection. At the same time as the shape began to enlarge, its definition became more clear, and it moved towards the window at a rate of stunning velocity. An arch bridge raging like a fireball was moving towards Rico's bedroom window and on top of the arch curve, he shockingly saw the vision of several faces, all with different expressions. Disir and Clytie burst back in and were forced inadvertently against the old door with a sudden jolt rendering their bodies motionless. Rico lifted his left arm, his finger shakily pointing at the extraordinary flaming vision beaming from outside the window. His jaw dropped as though weighted with lead and he found himself silently counting to himself the number of faces coming towards him. Sinking deeper into his being, bypassing with speed any emotions in the way so that he could remain still and soak in the reality of the spectacle, Rico noticed that one of the faces was too similar to that of his grandfather, Molecular McTyde.

Rico's heart was now pounding at fast staccato pace, an excitable wave of curiosity passed through him so he dared to whisper louder than before, "For the sake of Evaki, can you see those faces? Look, seven of them at least staring at us from under that arch bridge?" Before stunned Disir and Clytie could answer, a large explosion ripped through the bedroom, the window glass shattering into millions of pieces. All seven visions were now in the bedroom on the inside of what was the window;

the flaming arch bridge remained buoyant on the outside.

One of the visions, two along from his familiar late grandfather's, then spoke in an eerily low, croaky, penetrating voice, offering its burning hand in friendship "Come." Rico slowly lifted his cautious but intrigued body off the soft duvet, nodded his head in approval and slowly walked just behind the vision towards the window. The other six images followed silently and the faint voices of Disir and Clytie in the background muttered half-heartedly "Can we come too?" but the words were lost amidst the splattering and crackling of the flames. They followed anyway.

Stepping onto the flaming arch bridge felt similar to how it might feel taking the first steps on the Moon, but hotter, so thought Rico momentarily. Cautiously, they all walked across the flaming arch bridge, suspended in the sky with all of Flamesborough County lit up underneath them like an artist's poetic landscape. A brief breath in time to soak in the beauty of the Valley below. They suffered from disbelief but were thankful that the flames did not burn them, the heat just made them sweat, along with the fear of uncertainty of their final destination.

After what seemed like seconds but was apparently years, they arrived at the end of the flaming arch bridge where a whole new planet awaited them. The ground was smouldering, the trees and bushes were burnt to cinders, the air simmered with the reek of garlic, stagnant oil, the smell of ancient, stale smoke and burnt diesel. The silence penetrated the noise of the flames from the flaming arch bridge now in the distance behind them as the dark, seething coal under their feet got crushed with every footstep.

"Where are we?" Disir braved a comment. The visions wouldn't answer. Instead they suddenly stopped in their tracks, their faces changing back to the original expressions first observed by Rico in his bedroom. A wave of what seemed like sudden rage passed over the one who had spoken earlier, this time her dirty, brown, teeth gritted intently, eyes hollow, black, deathly, her hair straggly and unkempt with a wonky fringe. White bubbles of saliva began to dribble out of the corners of her mouth, her breathing became more accentuated, more of a sucking notion rather than relaxed inhalation. Her long, wiry, grey tongue hung out of her frothy mouth, wriggling slowly across her bottom lip. Rico stepped forward shuffling slowly towards the vision, the other visions thrashed and hissed like impatient serpents or hungry hyenas. Disir and Clytie shuddered and hid behind Rico who had no choice but to rid this luring vision of contempt and pain. Just then, the vision similar to Rico's grandfather, stepped forward, grabbing the tormented creature around her neck from behind. She squealed like a piglet, thrashed around from side to side to try and throw off Molecular McTyde but his grip was too strong. She tried to sink her blunt, infected teeth into his arm but the heat pushed her away. Now on her knees, she begged for mercy for him to let go of strangling her. Molecular McTyde regained his balance, then boomed "Unlock the Bridge of Therapus so that all souls who cross it for redemption can be set free. Hand over the key to my grandson, Rico McTyde so that you may be forgiven for my death."

"Never!" squalled the treacherous savage. "It is mine!" She reached out to grab Rico's pyjama collar with such force, Molecular McTyde lost his grip, ending up with just a few strands of her black, greasy locks in his burning hands. Chortling under her breath, her lunge was so dramatic, she tripped on a piece of coal, fell flat on her face, the key flew out from underneath her cloak and landed at the feet of Disir. Rico signalled to Disir to pick it but the uncontrollable, writhing beast had managed to regain herself upright. Pouncing at Disir who now had the key in her hand, she scratched the key out of Disir's hands, causing cuts and blood, and began running towards the bridge.

Molecular chased after her, but when she got to the face of the bridge, she halted, collapsed for the heat was too strong. The wreck now on the floor, wept. As Molecular slowed his pace and approached the heap, the convulsing spine spoke chapters of sorrow, remorse, regret. "Why did you kill me?" Molecular spoke calmly. There was no reply.

Rico came over and spoke, "I know grandfather. It is because you left without saying goodbye. It is because you spurned her offer to help you with your illness even though the ancient medicine men used to worship such gifts that she carries until the curse stepped in. It is because your love for her sister was greater than for her because she became cursed by the poison of the Ancient Sisiutl, the great double-headed snake, spirit of the waters, in the myths of The North American Indians and the Pacific." Molecular bent down and picked up the key off the burning ground, the sobbing finally ceased, the charred face of the dead spirit turned to look up at them both. Molecular reached out his hand, picked the body up off the floor, handed Rico the key. Rico moved towards the bridge, where he placed the key into a hole at the entrance, as he did so, he glanced one last time at his grandfather, stole a smile and Molecular and the redeemed brute disintegrated into powder.

It was time to head back across the bridge; the other faces moaned yearning for the key to redeem themselves and the end to their soul's misery. Rico summoned Disir and Clytie, he held the key between his fingers showing the faces he had it, nodded and promised in three words, "I'll be back." The heroic subjects turned, headed across the bridge and disappeared amongst the flames.

(From *The Haven Upper Realm Spirit Series*)

Bridge Passage
by Jane Pearn

The walk not finished, I stop to lean
on this barely-a-bridge spanning only
a grassy track. To what purpose the span?

For what reason my pause?
Warm brick hums beneath my forearms,
breeze riffles the backs of my legs.

Ochre cliffs a field away fall to a silken sea.
The tide is in. I watch the gulls' screams
tear strips off cobalt sky, leaving scrapes of white.

The bridge and I. In our shadows tall grasses ache with seed,
vetch embroiders their stems with purple.
Plump honeyed clovers, guarded by fierce nettles at the edge.

I stay although there is nothing much to see
because it is there, and I can,
and it may be the last time.

Life Span
by Ros Anderson

Seven-year old Callum was considered 'advanced for his years', especially by his mother. Others felt he was 'old before his time'. He didn't know exactly what people meant. He just wasn't that interested in football, which his classmates talked about all the time. He thought he'd like it better if his Dad was home to take him to matches. Callum kept looking at his Mum, wishing her tummy would grow, with a baby boy inside. A brother he could teach to make things. That's what he liked doing - designing and building. He was good at it. Mum said so. The teachers agreed. Dad told him the same, on rare occasions he was home.

Callum wondered if his Dad had become ... an 'absent father'. He had learnt the phrase from his mini computer, a present for his third birthday. He remembered Grandad was sad when he saw the gift and said, "Little boys need to explore to learn. When I was three I was always outside, making all sorts of things. I'm sure all that imagining, testing and discovering helped me become an engineer."

Callum remembered his Dad and Mum telling Grandad he was so 'last century'. "Tablets are the new way of exploring and this wee one is perfect for little hands," Dad had said. He remembered Grandad sighing and winking at Callum.

Grandad preferred books to screens. He encouraged Callum to explore the much-worn encyclopedia set which filled the middle shelf of the oak bookcase in his flat, which Mum called 'The Annexe'. Grandad called it 'The Old Man's Den'. Callum knew which sounded best. He loved snuggling into Grandad's shoulder, sitting in the Den, turning the pages to view beautiful coloured drawings and old photographs. One minute they would be looking at painted walls in an Egyptian tomb, and on the next page, fire bursting from the earth in a volcano. Each book packed with facts as well as songs and stories and with ten books in the set, boredom wasn't an option.

One day, soon after the discussion about the tablet, Grandad showed Callum the chapter on 'Bridges of the World'. There was so much information, alongside pictures of every type ever built, including the Forth Bridge, which Callum had seen once. He knew his Dad was a special adviser for the third Forth crossing. Callum hoped to see each stage being built but Dad was always too busy, too tired or working away, again. His Mum wasn't interested in seeing it before it was finished. She hoped to be at the grand opening wearing a new dress and fascinator. Callum wasn't really sure what one of those was. His Grandad had said it was bound to be something posh.

Callum and Grandad read together and talked about the differences between the bridges. Grandad was in his element. "I travelled to most of these during my training. Your Great Grandad worked hard to pay my fares. My lecturers said there was nothing like 'hands-on' learning' to make an engineer." Callum remembered his Dad talking about modern students viewing 'virtual' images of bridge constructions. Grandad seemed very dubious. "Seeing is believing," he said to Callum. "You can try and imagine how it might feel but until you're there, looking at the iron work, admiring the steel struts and massive steel cables, feeling the traffic or trains rumbling across, well, you really can't have the 'full picture'."

"Who built the first bridge, Grandad?" asked Callum.

"No-one knows but it probably happened as people travelled in search of food. To cross rivers someone would have tried larger and larger stepping stones, then added tree trunks and stone slabs. Gradually designs developed to produce footpaths in the air and designs grew bigger and grander all the time. The Romans managed to build the first arched bridges, without any computer-aided design of course!"

"Tell me more about local bridges, Grandad' said Callum. "Maybe Dad will take me to them next time he's home."

Callum thought Grandad looked sad again, but he livened up as he thought about suitable outings. "There are so many, Callum. The ones folks rush past or over everyday have so many stories to tell, like the Leaderfoot Viaduct and Lowood's Bottle Bridge. Then there's Rennie's Bridge in Kelso. John Rennie was the famous Scottish engineer who designed Waterloo Bridge for London. An Italian sculptor called it 'the noblest bridge in the world'. The Kelso bridge was really the prototype. I wonder what that Italian would have thought of our Union Chain Bridge, the oldest surviving iron suspension bridge in Europe. Rennie helped choose the winning design by Samuel Brown. It links Scotland and England and our famous River Tweed flows beneath. In 2020 it will be 200 years old. Let's hope we can be at the celebrations."

Callum thought the sad look was almost back, until Grandad spoke again. "You know, Callum, we could have a great outing to that bridge, with Dad *and* Mum." Callum looked doubtful. "Next door to the bridge," said Grandad, "is the Chain Bridge Honey Farm. I've noticed several books in your Mum's kitchen about the health benefits of honey.

I think she'd enjoy a visit. They even have special honey cake. Her book group might enjoy that." As an after-thought he said, "And on both bridge towers, linking a rose and thistle, are the Latin words, 'Vis Unita Fortior' which means 'United Strength is Stronger'. Maybe we'll take Uncle Gordon too."

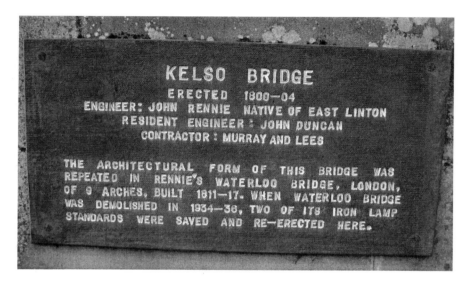

Gordon, Callum's musical Uncle, had said at a recent family gathering that he couldn't compete with the famous engineers of the family, but was himself 'a man of many bridges'. When Callum's Mum asked what on earth he was talking about, he directed his explanation at Callum. "Well there's the bridge on my fiddle, (which your Mum has to call a violin), and the one on my spectacles too. I've one for my snooker cue, for taking difficult shots and I'll show you that one day and teach you how to play." Callum's Mum winced. She thought that snooker was an awful game. Her game was tennis, which she played twice a week at a local hotel. Gordon continued: "I've got two bridges in my mouth as well. The dentist says that he can't add any more. My own fault, from too many sweets and fizzy drinks. Your Mum was much smarter of course, watching her weight, so she's got perfect teeth. She doesn't need bridges building, at least not in her mouth."

"That's enough," said Callum's Dad, "sometimes you just don't know when to stop, Gordon".

Later on, when Callum was about to read a bedtime story with his Mum, she had said, "Let Uncle Gordon's story about his dental bridges be a warning to you. It's hard to speak to someone with teeth like his." Callum nearly asked her if this was the only reason she didn't like speaking to Uncle Gordon, but stopped himself. Grandad had said a few times that she was 'very Edinburgh'. Callum wondered if he would understand family things more when he was a grown-up. He thought he would try and stick to bridges for now.

As usual, when Callum wanted to know more, he asked Grandad. "Why are all those things called bridges, which Uncle Gordon talked about? How can they all have the same name?"

"Well," said Grandad, "in the English language the same word can have different meanings, often with a link. 'Bridge' is an excellent example. All of Uncle Gordon's bridges are making connections. Some are probably working much harder than others."

"Like the ones in Uncle Gordon's mouth?" asked Callum, smiling.

"I expect so," said Grandad, "but think about the fiddle too. As the musician tightens each string, to tune the instrument, the bridge comes under even more strain. Sometimes they split and collapse. Just like some famous river and road bridges have over the years."

Then Grandad's sad look returned as he continued, "The word 'bridge' is also used in a way which is much harder to explain. It's the same idea about connecting things but about people and how they link together. One day something will help you to understand but you've got plenty more 'concrete' bridges to study for now." He chuckled to himself. Callum felt a bit confused about 'people bridges' and about studying 'concrete' bridges when he wanted to know much more about those made from iron and steel. He wondered if he wasn't as 'advanced' as people thought.

Whilst Callum learnt so much from his Grandad, he did also use his tablet. He watched programmes called soaps, which mentioned 'absent fathers' and one day he asked his Mum if his Dad was one of those. "Certainly not, Callum. He's a consultant engineer. He can be called out to any country in the world. Bridges could fall down without him. Imagine how awful that would be. Sometimes he is needed extremely urgently when bridges have already collapsed, after earthquakes and floods. He certainly hasn't left us. He's working hard to earn money. He wants to spend more time with us but something always crops up." Callum had heard on the tablet about things 'cropping up'. He knew it wasn't always about work. He must talk to Grandad.

Callum waited until Mum was busy baking for her next book group whilst trying to finish the latest book. She had just spilt the flour. She didn't notice him heading for Grandad, creeping down the stone-flagged passageway on tiptoe. The Annexe had been added when Granny Ellen died so that Mum and Dad could keep an eye on Grandad. Callum couldn't remember Granny but a striking black and white wedding photo showed her off in a gleaming silver frame in Grandad's entrance hall. Granny held an enormous bunch of flowers. Mum called it a bouquet. Grandad said, "Bouquet or bunch - it's all the same," and remembered all the flowers - pink roses and myrtle, white lilies, purple lavender, green sprigs of rosemary, tied with a blue silk ribbon. He had told Callum about brides having something blue, for good luck, and that these items often passed down through generations. One day, he had said, "Granny Ellen's blue ribbon is safely wrapped and if a little sister arrives for you Callum, she can use it on her wedding day". That meant Callum always felt a bit sad when he saw the photo. He really wanted the ribbon, being Grandad's first grandchild.

As he arrived at Grandad's door today though, he remembered why he was needing to talk. It wasn't about the ribbon. He always knocked and waited for the cheery, "Come away in". He heard nothing and knocked again. He thought perhaps Grandad was in the bathroom or on the toilet. Mum didn't ever seem to mention toilets. She only ever asked people if they needed the bathroom. What was wrong with saying toilet? It was another question for Grandad, but not today.

As Callum knocked again he heard an odd noise and decided to be brave and open the door. The wedding photo had disappeared. Around the corner Callum found Grandad, trying to hold the frame with one hand, the other flopped at his side. Callum remembered Grandad telling him sadly how he panicked when Granny Ellen collapsed and never forgave himself. Callum didn't hesitate. He grabbed Grandad's phone and dialled 999. As the lady questioned him, he told her Grandad's full name, George Andrew Murray and said, "I'm Callum and I'm looking after Grandad. I'm on my own with him."

"The paramedics will be with you very soon," the lady explained. "They'll check your Grandad and he'll probably go to hospital."

Grandad was trying hard to speak. Callum could hear a muffled 'bridge' amongst it all. He told the nice lady and proudly said, "My Grandad's a bridge expert. He used to be a civil engineer."

"Well," said the lady, "I expect you're his trainee. The ambulance and paramedics will be his 'bridge' to the hospital where the team will connect up, like one big bridge, to help him. Callum liked this idea but was thinking how cross Mum would be if her cake burnt and how angry

Dad might be if something had 'cropped up' and he was called home. The calm lady suddenly sounded different when she said firmly, but still kindly, "Don't you worry, Callum. I'm sure your Mum and Dad will be very proud of all you've done".

As he realised that he had been 'thinking out loud,' like Mum sometimes did, his Mum flew through Grandad's door, shouting "Callum, what's happening?" ahead of two paramedics. She saw Grandad and hugged Callum so hard he thought he would burst, as he still clung tightly to the phone.

"Is that your Mum now, Callum?" he heard down the line. Callum felt Grandad's hand move.

"Yes but I was looking after Grandad in The Old Man's Den." His Mum took the phone.

"I was in the main house not with them in 'The ...... Annexe'." Then, with a strained voice, she continued, "Or, as Callum said, not with them in 'The Old Man's Den'. I wasn't far away. We're altogether now. Thank you very much for your help." Callum thought the nice lady was trying to say something as his Mum put the phone down.

As the paramedics wheeled Grandad down the passageway, one of them winked at Callum, saying, "That's a great name for Grandad's place. I reckon a nice picture of it would cheer him up." Callum saw his Mum open her mouth to say something but closed it quickly. He was sure she was going to do that 'thinking out loud' thing as well, but stopped in time. He would get on with the picture and label it 'The Old Man's Den' in very large letters. Maybe Grandad could hang it on his front door when he came home.

The Bridge at Gordon Woodland
by Vee Freir

On this December morning, sun low
at the simple wooden structure
no less testament to man's ingenuity
than the contrailed sky.

air hoar tinges the bridge
makes the grass verge a white coral reef
as Eden Water rushes under
breaking against rocks and reeds

nothing else seems to stir
then a pair of ears appear
a roe deer, then another and another
until five heads are trained on me

I stay still
short burst
breath vapour
gives away my excitement

a twitch of ears and
still watching, wander off
into the frozen brush.
The river rustles on.

A day in the life
by Toni Parks

The three ladies wore black.

Not a conscious decision, just plain chance. Anyone discreetly observing them may have assumed a funeral was in the offing, far from it.

The three had met at 12.30 to celebrate a birthday, a milestone actually. On that day Anne, the youngest of the trio, was thirty years young. Even though there were not that many years between all three, the other two were envious of her youth but put on brave faces, masked by expensive cosmetics.

Another discreet observer may have pegged them as sisters with their beauty, posture, composure and mannerisms mirroring one another. Again, far from it, these three friends just enjoyed, and made the most of their time together by planning their rendezvous meticulously.

Confidence oozed from their very pores as stilettos clicked in unison, across the raw hewn wooden floor, beating out a staccato tattoo whilst the ladies angled towards the reserved table by the bay window. The best table in the restaurant and again planned. The vista presented was picturesque; a grassed area stretching out over 100 metres and bordered on its far perimeter by a gentle river, that birthday day glistening in the sunlight as it glided mesmerisingly slowly under a charming hump back bridge, winking on its way through the weeping willows that studded the near bank and curtsied in the slight breeze. Of course, the grassed area was teaming with al fresco diners, fidgeting and talking loudly, as they sat uncomfortably on the rustic outdoor furniture but that couldn't be helped. These girls were indeed meticulous but they had no control over the weather, especially from two weeks in advance when the booking had been made. So the exceptional dog-day warm spell brought out the crowds too, such was life.

"Well Anne," said Lottie, glass in hand, "the big three-oh, congratulations." Emily joined in as the three glasses came together with a satisfying chink in mid air.

"Yes, thank you both, I'm so glad we could all make it. But look at us, anyone would think we're off to a funeral rather than celebrating my birthday!" replied Anne.

"With me being four years older some days I feel like a walking funeral," quipped Lottie.

"Lottie! How can you say that? You're beautiful. If only my skin were so perfect. I'd die to know your secret. Whoops, sorry, that funeral theme again."

The friends paused in concentration as each one studied their menu, comfortable in the silence of each other's company. Emily produced a pair of specs from her clutch bag, all the better to study the specials on the blackboard. Anne read unflustered through her bifocal soft contacts, whilst Lottie, the eldest, just used the two eyes she had been born with. Deliberations and sighs eventually brought decisions. The fifteen-minute wait before the arrival of the starters allowed for a quick catch up on work, children, hobbies, and most importantly, sex life. And to be honest, some of it made for dull listening, although not all.

Eventually the starters arrived and the thrill or horror of possibly being two months late, baby teething, and the price of eggs were replaced with man talk, be it husband or partner. Husband for Lottie and Anne, partner for Emily, not being big on convention. All three had lived with their respective partners for between seven and ten years, and all three had complained of their respective partners' itches on more than one occasion. Lottie's main beef always revolved around money and the lack of it. With neither one being on a high enough salary to suit Lottie's lifestyle, Dave constantly monitored her spending and controlled her access to their joint finances. It wasn't all one way she had remarked with a smirk referencing the black number she was wearing as being the trade off for favours in the bedroom. The two friends *tsssked* in sympathy and solidarity, in acknowledgment to the true wearer of the trousers.

Emily had no such problem, not with money anyway, and in light of communication difficulties bedroom favours didn't sit high on her list of activities either. The problem she did have though was with Paul's lack of understanding, concern or commitment for their two young children. Sure his salary financed the majority of the child minder fees, which allowed Emily to continue working and so feel part of the human race but apart from the occasional walk with the double buggy he spent most of his free time watching football or being out with his friends, either at the gym or in the pub. She looked accusingly at her friends but both shook their heads in unison inferring that he didn't really mix with their other halves.

"Where's he today then? If you're here, who's looking after the two girls?" asked Anne, now feeling guilty at having dragged Emily away from her family duties.

"Oh, it's OK. He's got them today, football's away this week and with the weather being nice he's taking them out. No doubt at some point he'll bump into his mates though."

Anne was about to continue the conversation when the waiter arrived to take away used plates. It gave her time to firm up on her gripes about Roger. A pregnant pause suddenly descended on the table, only to be rescued by a top up of Verve Cliquot. Talking of children and pregnant pauses she was unsure whether to be happy or not at the omen of being late. Both her mind and eyes continued to drift out across the field to the river and then on, to the listed bridge that had been a mainstay of the village since the early 19th century, and no doubt the reason why the village had grown so. Emily touched her lower arm by way of advising her that the waiter wished to place down her main course.

"Sorry, miles away. Well not that far really, just the other side of the bridge but you know what I mean," said Anne, in a wistful voice. Lottie reminded her that Roger was the next subject on their agenda.

"Yes, Roger," she began as her fork hovered over a pork medallion. "I was just thinking we're sat here like three wise monkeys but when it comes to 'speak no evil' we do nothing but; do we? We may all look the part but we certainly don't act it. Anyway, yes about Roger. What can I say? For starters, I certainly think he's got the seven year itch."

The other two looked aghast. "But it's not for another woman, it's for me. He's being particularly attentive towards me, buys me flowers and other little gifts."

"What like?" they asked together with eyes twinkling.

"Lingerie, chocolates, books … but having said all that we did row this morning."

"You rowed? On your birthday? But you never row," they said together.

"I know but I was looking forward to meeting up with you two and wearing my new dress and all. And he wanted something else. You know that Saturday morning togetherness."

"You mean sex, right," said a forthright Lottie, with a knowing look.

"Yes, I mean sex. I said no, sorry, it's a shower and me time, and as you girls know when you reach thirty, me time takes that little bit longer."

Both looked daggers at her but knew she was right.

"Then he went on about the fact I was going for a meal and a drink at lunchtime when he was planning to take me out tonight. And I said, it's not the same. And he said, it costs money the same, though. And I said, so does that bloody Kawasaki. Go ride that!"

Lottie's and Emily's forks dangled in space as each mouthed questioningly to the other, 'Kawasaki'. Anne had blindly continued by adding that it was 1000cc too, so the fuel and insurance didn't come cheap either, and that ended her bitch. Well, not quite as she rounded off with, "It's a Japanese motorbike, all shiny chrome and bright colours. Makes a hell of a din when he revs it."

"So is that what he did?" asked Emily.

"Think so. He was putting on his black leathers as I was squeezing into this," she answered, running her hand down the side of her little black dress. "I nearly caved though, he did look cute and butch at the same time once he was clad all in leather but I was running late anyway. So he went off with a bee in his helmet and I came here feeling just a teeny bit guilty and more than a little bit horny to boot."

The sound of Emily's phone chime broke into their laughter forcing her to make two decisions. One, not to check the text message and two, to say, "Good one, Anne. I think we better order more champagne and celebrate in style. It will really wind him up and perhaps that way some of your glow might rub off on the rest of us," as she tried to catch the waiter's eye.

To confirm his disappointment Roger put a full stop on the conversation by flipping down his visor, never noticing the slight pang of desire in Anne's eye. He stormed out of the house leaving the door ajar and, as suggested, rode his bike. The busy main street ensured slow progress but an open, although narrow road beckoned beyond the derestricted speed limit zone. Soon his vision was troubled by intermittent rays of sunshine dappling through the autumn leaves from canopy above. His concentration level increased to compensate and his pace slowed even more.

Paul's physical exertion at buggy pushing brought about an unpleasant clammy sensation not to his liking. His tether end had already been reached when the twins had caused a tizz by decorating the kitchen floor with their pasta shapes lunch, but given the warm fresh air they were now thankfully asleep. He deliberated over his mental anguish and decided to take the bull by the horns and text. He walked slowly as his fingers felt their way across the buttons of his mobile. With its despatch came a sense of relief and advancement to Robbie's flat.

The smile on Dave's face mimicked the width of the Forth Bridge. Saturday morning sex, he almost believed it was his birthday not Anne's. He marvelled at how lucky he was as he had watched Lottie pour herself into that dress, which must have been at least two sizes too small. Perhaps, small is cheaper, he thought. He had showered and dressed just in time to wave her off, in fact her Angel perfume still lingered on his T-shirt. The rest of the day is going to be an anti-climax now, he mused. Checking out the fridge he settled on an all-day breakfast at the village café instead.

Upward of an hour astride his bike and buffeted by what little breeze condescended to slow his progress Roger's brain mapped out a mental route home. Travelling at speed had cleared away any angst that had been allowed to manifest itself, so the homeward journey along the side of the Teviot was undertaken at a more sedate pace.

Robbie had welcomed Paul with open arms and was even more effusive on hearing of his decision. The twins unwoken by their buggy manhandling up the stairs to Robbie's flat were unable to witness their father kissing and embracing another man. Their little ears would soon be enlightened as to his proposed plans anyway, but just not quite yet. Paul's text to Emily had lit the blue touch paper so all that remained was for him to face the fireworks. He took Robbie's leave and headed back, probably for the last time, to the house he had called home choosing the scenic route over the narrow bridge.

Dave, on leaving the café, ventured over to the car boot sale on the Green. He mosied around table after table of other folks' junk and cast offs, and although not productive at least it whiled away an hour. His most direct route home took him over the village's old stone bridge. Not really suited to today's traffic it operated a priority one-way traffic light system, only today the lights were out. Taking particular care he hugged the parapet to give any traffic, in either direction, as clear a run as possible. He nodded a greeting, as he was about to pass Robbie and the twins coming the other way. Robbie returned it with a mouthed acknowledgment lost to the roar of a motorbike.

Celebration over, the three friends drained their glasses and studied the bill. A minor skirmish ensued where first Anne took charge of the payment and then the other two wrestled it out of her hands. Peace was restored with Anne and Lottie popping to the loo for a comfort break and face fix leaving Emily to deal with the finances. This gave her a chance to pull out her mobile and check that message, which had begun playing on her mind. A terrific squeal of tyres and sickening screech of grinding metal quickly followed by a splash shocked her in to dropping the mobile even as she swiped the screen. The sound automatically directed her gaze towards the bridge and river where smoke and steam were now pervading the air. Bodies, both inside and out, all turned in unison toward the unexpected noise, as if hypnotised. Eyes focused on the bridge in expectation of still further action. Snippets of possible names of those involved were bandied about as recognition set in. Lottie and Anne rushed to Emily's side, both desperate to know what had happened. She seemed transfixed by a tragedy that was over before she'd almost become aware of it.

But tragedy it was. Roger, driving steadily and warily on his Kawasaki followed Dave onto the bridge. With no stop signal to advise otherwise a car approached from the opposite direction and at speed. Only once over the hump did the driver perceive his foolishness, by which time a collision with Paul and the buggy was inevitable. Dave could see the danger playing out too but Paul was oblivious as he was facing away from the oncoming car.

Paul was shocked by Dave's actions when both the twins and he were forcefully pushed further into the side of the wall. A rush of air, a dull thud and metallic scream resulted a split second afterwards all adding to Paul's confusion, and concluded with a splash as a motorcyclist somersaulted over the bridge side and into the river. Shock took hold of the onlookers. An eerie silence fell, only to be broken moments later by the cries of young children.

Any mother would have reached out and physically felt their pain and Emily was no exception. She grabbed instinctively for her mobile, more to ensure Paul and the girls were not in the vicinity to witness such a horror. A text message halted her momentum. *He was leaving for another. A man?* Hands pawed at her arms whilst confusion prevented her brain from functioning, as Anne and Lottie both mouthed unintelligible words in her direction. Tears streamed from their freshly made up eyes, eyes that had not only observed the accident but had also recognised those they thought involved, cruelly confirmed by their loved ones' names being murmured over and over amongst an ever increasing throng.

Two men died and the car driver was taken into police custody.

The man pushing the buggy escaped with minor cut and bruises.

The two children in the buggy were shaken up by the episode but otherwise unhurt.

The three ladies wore black.

The Graven Image!
by Heather Bolton

I met a man

a face of stone

expressionless

far from home.

He took the facts

full in the face

contorted them,

he had no grace –

spreading, great big

whopping lies –

his face grew graven –

caught now

forever

in course stone!

No roving, anymore

from home

'Bridge' by definition
by Gwen Chessell

The word 'bridge' holds within its concept a multitude of meanings. It can be a noun, a verb or an adjective. But however it performs grammatically, it also signifies something comfortable, something positive, a safeguard, the remedy to a problem. It can provide a solution in so many situations. In its commonest usage, it spans a gap, a space between two points, usually but not exclusively, over running water – it is two-way – a starting point and a finishing point. And so it 'bridges' a gap. A bridge can be a causeway, an aqueduct, a viaduct, a railway, a pontoon, a bridge of boats, a drawbridge over the moat of a castle and so on. It is a connection, a conduit.

The first bridge, in the obvious sense of the word, was dreamt up by our ancient forefathers to ease their hunting and gathering forays and was probably a chance fallen tree. It must have seemed to the first hunter-gatherers so obvious a solution that it was inevitable that they would seize axe and rope and go on to construct their own simple structures. Most bridges continued to be made of wood, but as time went on, structures of stone appeared that incorporated learnt building features such as arches and parapets. Inevitably came those, like the Romans, who using previous knowledge of construction and geology, executed their structures in stone; some of these bridges would survive for a millennium or more. Then came the old stone bridges of the middle ages, with their often hump-backed outlines heaving themselves over the gap. These evoke particular reflection and affection. An example is the late 15th century bridge over the River Almond at Cramond. One thinks of kings and courtiers and men of high degree, crossing the bridge on horseback or on foot as they went between Edinburgh and Queensferry. Some time would elapse though before the age of stone bridges moved on to those built by sophisticated engineering techniques, using materials such as iron and steel. These would lead to the development of impressive edifices, often of arresting beauty and marvellous creativity. Will the newest bridge over the Forth give us delight as well as satisfaction in its design?

The factor that over-rides anything else contained in the very concept of a bridge is safety. So when something occurs which turns the comfort implicit in a bridge's intrinsic meaning into a negative, the gap a bridge is supposed to vanquish triumphs over the solution. This can have shocking and tragic consequences. Bridges require an investment of know-how; what materials to use for the task a structure will perform, what design will fulfil its purpose best and what will fit the landscape in which the bridge will sit. Men have paid a price in building bridges, not just in money, hard graft and sweat but also in tearful sacrifice. The Forth Rail Bridge, a cantilever bridge that has World Heritage listing and is hailed as a wonder of the modern world is, perhaps, one of the most successful and praiseworthy crossings ever built. But even so, its construction towards the end of the 19th century was to demand the cost of 79 lives, most of these before it was even completed. Earlier in the same century the Tay Bridge fell victim to human incompetence, bad design, and shoddy materials. As a train crowded with passengers crossed the wide wild water of the River Tay, the bridge collapsed beneath it. It plunged to the depths taking with it those who had placed their lives, on that stormy, gale-tossed December night, in the supposed safety of its structure. This last tragedy still invites remembrance as one crosses the Tay and the pitiful remnants of the piers of the original ill-fated span march side by side for a while with the newer and safer replacement. On the many occasions when our family travelled south by rail from our home in Aberdeenshire, the approach to the bridge was anticipated in sombre mood. The children gazed out of the carriage window at the water washing against the visible stumps, mentally digesting the facts they already knew so well. Further questions were always the same, questions which only morbid imagination could answer.

So much for physical bridges, each of us holds within us a more personal, cerebral kind of bridge. This is the bridge of memories, a solace in these days of encroaching age and creeping decrepitude. The gap between the present and many years past can be banished by calling up a scintilla, a spark of recall from the kaleidoscope of images that we hold within our minds. Within this there is another bridge, the bridge between memory and what really happened. We all remember the past differently and our memories are often faulty, they have gaps where reality has fallen through the cracks. But the gaps can be bridged by imagination. Perhaps this kind of bridge is not as secure as a well-built physical bridge but it still offers comfort—a remedy for those experiencing a regretful yearning for lost youth.

Reflections from the Bridge
by Patricia Watts

It was December 28th, 1912. Captain Thomas Mcintyre stood on the bridge of his ship casting his eye over the calm waters as he brought his beloved vessel into the harbour for the last time. It had been a hard decision but his wife was not in good health and needed his support. There was a great deal of political strife in Europe too and if there was to be a war, God forbid, he thought a younger person would need to be at the helm. To the port side, the stumps of the piers that had supported the girders of the original rail bridge ran alongside the second one. They were a stark reminder of the catastrophe that had befallen the first rail bridge some thirty odd years ago. He reflected on this disaster in which so many had lost their lives. Fate played a mixed hand that day.

***

It was the 28th of December 1879. Tommy sat with his legs dangling over the wharf. He turned his head at the sound of a familiar whistle. The sun was bright in his eyes but he knew it was Jimmy kicking loose stones and scuffing towards him.

"Hello pal. What's up? Why yer looking so miserable? Anyway, shouldn't you be in Church. It's Sunday."

Tommy turned his gaze across the water again. He loved the hubbub, the hustle and bustle and noise of the Dundee docks, the sirens of the large cargo ships as they were skilfully steered into the harbour with their heavy loads of jute; their smoke stacks belching black smoke. Watching the Broughty Ferry cross the river and the pleasure paddle steamers as they puddled around the coast. This was his favourite pastime. It was quieter today; today being the Sabbath.

"I couldn't go to see grandmother with mother and sister yesterday, cos I had a fever. I did so want a ride on the train over the bridge. Never been before. I'm s'posed to be indoors but I was bored. Father told me I shouldn't be down here mixing with all the ragamuffins so if he finds out he'll get his 'tawse out again."

"You been answering back agin, then?"

"Yes, argued about leaving school. He knows I want to join the Merchant Navy to be a captain of a cargo ship and that I don't wa'n na be a school master like him with the Presbytery always on ma back. He's already found a Pupil Teacher post for me."

"Huh, wish I could go to school, but no chance. Have to help me Ma in the jute factory. I'm sick of gettin' choked with dust and muck. Since Da had the accident unloadin' bales of jute there's not been much money. He's a 'kettle biler' now and s'posed to look after the bairns but he's always drunk. There's six mouths to feed and another on the way. We didn't have nothing for Christmas. Bet you did. I don't know what's gonna happ'n."

"That's no good Jimmy. Where's Martha, that bonnie sister of yours? She's not been around for a few days."

"She's helpin' in the factory too. Has to clear up all the dust from them machines."

"Father says it should all be stopped because ther'll be a serious accident one o' these days and all bairns should be in school anyway but there's not enough money for the Board to do their job properly."

"Well he would say that."

Tommy skimmed a few pebbles across the water, then springing to his feet said, "Goin' home to get m'dinner. Tell Martha I'll be down later to watch the ferry cross."

That afternoon, Tommy watched the ferry cross the river and return at its usual time of quarter past four. The sun was shining and there was hardly a ripple on the water. Martha was waiting for him.

"Haven't got long Tommy. Should have brought wee George with me but Jimmy says he'll mind him for a bit."

Tommy and Martha watched the ferry come in at the jetty. They laughed and joked for a while but Martha shivered in her thin, ragged dress. Tommy felt sorry for her. He was very fond of Martha. He thought she deserved a better life than looking after her young brothers. When she wasn't doing that she was in that filthy factory.

"Here have my jacket to put round yer shoulders. Wind seems to be gettin' up."

"Ta but I best be goin' home now."

"Oh well I'll walk you to the end of your street then."

Tommy gingerly placed his arm around her shoulder pulling her close to stop her from shivering as they walked towards the block of tenement flats that was her home. He thought how cold and uninviting they looked.

He knew he would be in trouble if his father found out where he had been. He slipped quietly upstairs to his room. Later he called to his father who was poring over his papers, as usual, on a Sunday, "What time's

Mother comin' home?"

"The train's expected at about half past seven. We'll take the horse and carriage down to the station to meet them."

***

On this same day in that dreary tenement block close to the jute factory, Beth read and reread the letter that had arrived from London a week ago. Her hands trembled every time she removed it from the envelope.

'... I will be arriving on the Edinburgh to Dundee train at half past seven on December 28th. I have told Mary my wife that I am coming on business but, of course, I have not alerted her to the fact that I will not be returning. I will make sure that she and the children are well provided for. I am longing to take you in my arms again and know that we will be happy together even though the accommodation you have found is modest. It will not always be thus I promise.

'It seems so long since you first came down and that night at the party when we all had so much to drink. Your aunt's demise has changed the whole course of our lives ...'

Beth had left her job in Dundee as a maid and had gone to London to look after a wealthy aunt who was not as wealthy as she had been given to believe. She had hoped this might be an escape from the drudgery to which there seemed to be no end but her vulnerability had been exploited.

"Wife, Mary," she muttered under her breath, "so he's already married then. Oh my God," she gasped as her hands continued to shake. This morning she had pulled the crumpled letter from her pocket and read it again. Her mother snatched it from her but she was unable to read it. Beth struggled but with help from a friend had managed to make sense of it.

"It doesn't mean a thing. If he comes it'll be 'cos he thinks you've some money and I bet you haven't told him about the bairn that's growing in yer belly, his bairn. See what he does when he finds out. Then you'll know his true colours. Should've known I couldn't trust you down there. Silly wench! And he a married man too! I don't know what the neighbours'll say."

***

Now Tommy's grandmother, Hettie, lived in a pretty little white painted cottage in Wormit on the south side of the Tay about ten minutes' walk from the station. The family loved to visit and the new bridge made it a lot easier for them. At 6.50, time for their return she walked to the station with her daughter and granddaughter to wave goodbye and anxious to see them safely on the train. Dark clouds thickened overhead and a strong wind was intensifying and gathering pace. When the train pulled in Hettie kissed her daughter fondly on the cheek and as she took her hand said, "Mind thee bring ma grandson Tommy, next time you come. Haste thee back and may God be with thee."

Then she turned to her granddaughter and ruffling her pretty fair curls said, "Now hen, make sure you look after your mother."

She wiped a tear from her eye as they stepped on to the train and waved them out of the station. Hettie watched until the train was out of sight but as she turned a fierce gust of wind took her hat and the bridge seemed to be swinging from side to side being strained to its limits with the force of the gathering wind. Hettie was terrified and worried for her family.

**

Eliza Merryweather was waiting, with her mother and father, to board the train in London on that fateful day, too. A station assistant took charge of her large portmanteau and hatboxes. She removed her hands from her muff, embraced her parents and gave them each a kiss. She was going to take up a position with one of the shipbuilding magnates, in Dundee, as a nanny to the children who had lost their mother in childbirth. "Goodbye and don't worry about me," she called as she stepped on to the train.

Her mother turned to her father, "I knew Eliza would do well for herself and who knows she could end up marrying her boss."

Despite her excitement Eliza was apprehensive. One or two of the rougher types of men who had boarded at Edinburgh eyed her up and down. They looked as though they were labourers or fishermen returning to work after spending Christmas with their families. She shuffled nearer the window and gazed at the passing countryside to avoid their leering advances.

That evening the Edinburgh train pulled out of the station on time, fully laden with passengers returning to Dundee for various reasons. It also pulled a wagonload of mailbags.

Dave Finlay was the engine driver who was to take the train to Dundee that night and his mate Jock was on the footplate stoking the fire. Dave was looking forward to having a couple of glasses of beer before going home to his wife and family. It had been a long day but he did not complain about the long hours. He had been newly promoted and was thankful that the bridge had brought fresh opportunities for them.

By the time the train had reached the last station on the south side of the bridge the clouds overhead were black and menacing. The storm raged through the estuary but nevertheless, clearance to cross the bridge was given by the signalman, at 7.15, on time, and in turn the signalman at the Dundee end had been alerted. The engine whistled as the train approached the bridge, which was swaying violently. The passengers were being lurched from side to side. Beneath, the waters were being whipped into a maelstrom. Some of the passengers must have anticipated that this could be their final crossing.

The rail bridge was still relatively new and intrigued many people who watched in awe as the trains chugged majestically, high over the water. Tonight was no exception. All the folk who had gathered to meet relatives or friends clung to each other in an effort to withstand the force of the wind and the lashing rain. They strained their eyes to watch the lights, almost obliterated by the weather, of the incoming train as it made its way through the inky blackness but then, as it took the curve, it vanished. Those waiting stood agape in disbelief. Screams rent the bitter night air as they began to realise what must have happened. Word soon spread that the train had not reached the other side of the bridge. It was later established by station personnel that a section of the bridge had, indeed, collapsed. The train had been swallowed by the raging waters of the Tay.

***

The months passed. There was a bleakness in the air which did not lift with the coming of spring. There was a sense of a terrible void in the whole community. This disaster and the loss of life (there were no survivors) had catastrophic consequences for the relatives and families of those who were travelling on that fateful day. There was much wringing of hands at the coincidences. Families were bereft of their loved ones and their breadwinner; many widows were left with young families and stricken with poverty in one fell swoop. Mail continued to be washed up on the shores for weeks after the event.

Tommy spent more and more time down on the docks.

"How's yer father taking it Tommy? I've heard he's in a bad way?"

Tommy skimmed stones over the water. He did not look up. He knew it was Jimmy. "Ah well, he took to drink and lost his job didn't he. Beats me for the smallest thing. Think he wishes it'd been me on the train," he said. "Grandmother dying of a broken heart so soon after. He just couldna take it." The stones jumped and splashed across the water as Tommy vented his anger.

"What'll you do then?"

"I'm going to join the Merchant Navy as a trainee. That's what I've always wanted to do and father won't stop me now. He just doesn't care any more."

"You know that Beth who lived not far from us, close to the factory. Well she lost her fancy man from the train. He was s'posed to be coming to marry her and they say her mother went into a rage. She threw Beth out, said she didn't have enough money to keep her and another bairn. Had her baby in some home. Never saw it and now they say she's on the streets."

Mary eventually discovered that her husband had lost his life but of course, was never aware of her husband's infidelity. Although she had been left with money she was now a widow and her children fatherless.

Eliza Merryweather's parents were distraught and blamed themselves for letting her go so far away, despite the fact there were few or no other opportunities for their daughter.

***

As Captain Thomas Mcintyre arrived home, his wife Martha was there to greet him.

While he was growing up he had always rebelled against his father, who had long since died a broken man; his religious upbringing and their opposing views but today he offered a silent prayer of thanks.

Contributors

Ros Anderson - After a career as an NHS clinical pharmacist working across the UK, during which I was involved in factual writing for academic texts and journals, I am now exploring my creative side. I built confidence on an excellent Creative Writing Course at Borders College, trying my hand at a short story, fairytale, and pieces for stage and screenplay. Now a regular participant in the Border Writers' Forum and the Kelso Writers' Group, both of which provide creative stimulation via guest speakers and fellow members. Non-academic publications: 'A Sense of Train' in BWF Anthology 2015.

Have to mention my one success in a creative writing competition: The Southern Reporter Spooky Story competition December 2014!

Heather Bolton - I have no claim of being a poet with a capital "P". My approach is as long-term appreciative reader from an early age. It is about finding relevant meaning. My writing is about expressing this as succinctly, simply and enjoyably as I can.

Antony Chessell has published a historical biography, *The Life and Times of Abraham Hayward, Q.C.* and edited a World War II diary. Other books have a local theme, *Coldstream Building Snippets*, *The Braw Trees of Coldstream*, *Leet Water: From Source to Tweed* and *Breamish and Till: From Source to Tweed*. www.antonychessell.co.uk

Gwen Chessell - former medical educationist, Gwen has written three historical biographies and is just finishing the fourth. She spends most of her thinking time in the 19th century. For further information see her website: www.gwenchessell.co.uk

Oliver Eade - A retired doctor, and writer of novels, short stories and plays, in his YA *From Beast to God* trilogy, Oliver explores the different realities of Native American and European beliefs. The bridge they cross connects modern America, where the writer once worked, with the resurrected girl's ancestral past.

Hayley M. Emberey has enjoyed writing for seventeen years for study, stimulus, healing, discovery and advancement into other realms of thought, spirit, where the scope to write becomes boundless rather than restricted. The 'Bridges' theme immediately created the vision of the joining of two worlds dependent on each other for survival and progress and the Bridge of Therapus is to be their only hope.

Keith Farnish - a writer, serial volunteer, music promoter, bushcraft teacher, homemaker and IT expert who lives in St Boswells. He has had two non-fiction books about the environmental crisis published, and has written three novels to date. As far as bridges are concerned, all life is concerned with change, and all change needs a little help over it.

Vee Freir is a seven-eighths retired clinical psychologist, who started writing poetry when she came to the Scottish Borders from the Highlands in 2008. She also writes non-fiction books and her latest book 'Learn To Stress Less' can be found on Amazon.

Pamela Gordon Hoad had a career in public service and is now involved with various voluntary groups but she is also concentrating on her writing. She published two historical thrillers in 2016 (*The Devil's Stain* and *The Angel's Wing*). *The Cherub's Smile* is due for publication later in 2017.

Naomi Green - I have written prose and poetry in bits and bobs for many years, though I constantly languish in the guilt of under-achievement - children's fault! I wrote this on a train journey. The idea of 'falling in' with someone on such a journey intrigued me. I teach English as a Foreign Language, and like stories with an international flavour.

Anita John – This poem was written as part of the Storied Landscape Project 2015 for Abbotsford House/CABN following a walk from Huntly Burn to Abbotsford, the former home of Sir Walter Scott. Anita is currently Writer in Residence for RSPB Scotland Loch Leven, helping the reserve to celebrate and document its 50th anniversary. http://anitajohn.co.uk/

Bridget Khursheed - This poem was inspired by a sleeper bridge found on the old railway line through Gordon Moss. This section between Earlston and Duns closed after a week's heavy rain culminated in a violent rainstorm late on 12th August 1948. Watercourses "overtopped their banks into ground already saturated; resulting in multiple washouts of railway embankments and undermining of bridge abutments and piers". The passenger service never re-opened, but a goods train between St Boswells and Greenlaw resumed after a period; running until 19 July 1965.

Robert Leach - a former chair of Borders Writers' Forum. He has been working at the craft of poetry for nearly fifty years, and has published four collections and nine chapbooks. He is also a theatre practitioner and historian, who has worked in USA and Russia, and published eight theatre books. His ninth, a history of British theatre, will be published in 2018.

Tom Murray - I've always equated bridges real or metaphorical with writing. The crossing into new or familiar territory always throws up the unexpected. Each journey offering differing perspectives because you are not the same person. You notice the unfamiliar or see the familiar in a different light.

Toni Parks – my usual style of writing is Borders noir. This particular story portrays the light and dark of life, what you see and don't, and how quickly you can be robbed, at a stroke, by fate's fickle hand. Gardening, helping with the care of my grandson, household maintenance and chauffeuring are great levelers, making me realise storytelling's all, just in my head. Also, BWF secretary, for my sins.

Jane Pearn writes poems and short stories. She moved to the Borders in 2005 and has felt at home ever since. She has a special affection for bridges, real and metaphorical, and views writing as a way to try to bridge the gap between minds.

Laurna Robertson - A visit to Lindisfarne is dependent on the tide level at the causeway. There is a sense of anticipation because I never know what I will find on the island. On this occasion in St Mary's Church I found Fenwick Lawson's wooden sculpture of six monks carrying Cuthbert's coffin.

Raghu Shukla - A remorseful event, etched in my mind, inspired me to write this article. While in New York in 1989 for a two-week lecture-cum-study tour, my plan to visit the world-famous Brooklyn Bridge along with colleagues from Mount Sinai Hospital, was hijacked by a medical college friend of mine who persuaded me, instead, to visit his home.

Margaret Skea - Published writing includes two award-winning Scottish historical novels, *Turn of the Tide* and *A House Divided,* and a short story collection, *Dust Blowing and Other Stories.* The light-hearted story featured here was written purely for fun, inspired by the bridge (pictured), which sits in the middle of a field near Ancrum.

Gillian Vickers - I write to express myself and hope that someone can relate to it or even like it! I had writer's block when it came to writing on 'Bridges' until I realised I don't really like them, at least big metal ones, then the words flowed like a babbling brook.

Patricia Watts - My foray into writing commenced with children's stories. I joined Kelso Writers concentrating on short stories two of which have been published in the Eildon Tree. 'Reflections on the Bridge' was inspired by reading accounts of the Tay Bridge disaster. I have just completed the first draft of a novel.

Aims

- ➢ To promote interest and raise the profile of contemporary local writers
- ➢ To provide a focus for writing-related events in the Scottish Borders
- ➢ To provide networking opportunities
- ➢ To support professional development through talks, regular readings and workshops
- ➢ To offer fellow writers a friendly and supportive environment

Borders Writers' Forum meets monthly between September – June.

Further details, including a programme of events, available on: www.borderswritersforum.org.uk